THE UNIFIED PROJECT MANAGER

A QUICK REFRESHER FOR PROJECT MANAGERS

PUNEET SEHGAL

To my loving family - My Parents, Loving Wife (Priyanka), Sister (Vandana Malhotra), Brother-in-law (Vikas Malhotra), Maira Sehgal , Juana Sehgal , Tanya Malhotra, and Dev Malhotra

Your unwavering support has been the cornerstone of my journey in mastering project management. Through countless late-night study sessions and your encouraging words of wisdom, you have been my rock. This book is a testament to your belief in me and the sacrifices you've made. Thank you for being my constant source of inspiration and motivation.

To my mentors in the field of project management, who have inspired me to pursue excellence and share knowledge—your guidance has been instrumental in my growth.

To the countless project managers around the world, who tirelessly turn visions into realities—your dedication is admirable.

To the readers of this book, may it serve as a guide and inspiration on your journey to becoming exceptional project managers.

And to the leaders whose guidance and vision have shaped my career—your insights have been invaluable in navigating the complexities of project management. I am deeply grateful for the opportunity to learn from you and to continue growing under your mentorship.

With heartfelt gratitude,

Puneet Sehgal

Contents

Contents

Copyright Page

Foreword

In today's dynamic business environment, mastering the fundamentals of project management is not just a skill but a strategic imperative. This book, penned by Puneet Sehgal, is a comprehensive guide born from years of firsthand experience and a deep understanding of what it takes to succeed in project execution.

As someone who has witnessed the transformative power of effective project management, I can attest to its pivotal role in driving organizational success. This book not only demystifies the complexities of project management but also equips readers with practical tools and strategies to navigate challenges and seize opportunities.

Through clear and concise explanations, Puneet breaks down essential concepts, from initiating projects to managing stakeholders and delivering results. Whether you're a seasoned professional or new to the field, the insights shared here will empower you to lead with confidence and achieve measurable outcomes.

I commend Puneet for sharing their expertise in such a accessible and insightful manner. This book is not just a guide; it's a roadmap to excellence in project management. I encourage you to immerse yourself in its pages and discover how mastering these principles can propel your projects and your career forward.

Priyanka Khurana
Scrum Master
Adidas

Preface

When I embarked on the journey to become a certified Project Management Professional (PMP), I could never have anticipated the profound impact it would have on my career and personal growth. This book is the culmination of that journey, crafted with the intent to share the knowledge, experiences, and insights I've gathered over the years.

As a program and project manager with 18 years of experience, I have witnessed firsthand the transformative power of effective project management. From successfully leading transformation programs with a 98% success rate to navigating the complexities of Agile and Waterfall methodologies, my path has been both challenging and rewarding. Each project has taught me invaluable lessons, not just in managing tasks and teams, but in fostering collaboration, driving innovation, and delivering results that matter.

This book is dedicated to those who have supported me along the way—my family, whose unwavering faith in me was my constant source of strength, and the leaders and mentors who have guided and inspired me. It is their encouragement and belief in my potential that have fueled my passion for project management and motivated me to put pen to paper.

In these pages, you will find a comprehensive guide to the basics of project management, designed to be both practical and insightful. Whether you are new to the field or looking to refresh your knowledge, my goal is to provide you with a crisp solid foundation and practical tools that you can apply in your own projects.

As you read through this book, I invite you to reflect on your own journey, to embrace the challenges and opportunities that come your way, and to approach project management with a spirit of curiosity and resilience. My wish is that this book serves as a valuable resource, empowering you to lead with confidence, inspire your teams, and deliver projects that create lasting impact.

Thank you for joining me on this journey. I am excited to share my knowledge with you and look forward to hearing about your experiences and successes as you apply the principles outlined in these pages.

Warm regards,

Puneet Sehgal

Acknowledgements

Writing a book on project management basics has been a journey filled with learning, growth, and gratitude. I am deeply indebted to those who have supported and inspired me along the way.

First and foremost, I extend my heartfelt thanks to my family. Your unwavering support, patience, and understanding during countless hours of writing and research have been my anchor. I am endlessly grateful for your love and encouragement.

I would like to express my sincere appreciation to professors and cohort at **IIM Ahmedabad** for providing me with a transformative learning experience that has significantly enriched my understanding of management principles and project execution.

I would like to express my sincere appreciation to all the leaders from whom I have gained experience and knowledge about industry best practices, whose guidance and mentorship have been instrumental in shaping my career and approach to project management. Your insights and wisdom have been invaluable, and I am privileged to have learned from you.

To my colleagues and friends who provided feedback, encouragement, and moral support throughout this journey, thank you for believing in me and in the importance of sharing knowledge.

I am thankful to the organizations where I have contributed — Ericsson, British Telecom, Wipro Technologies, HCL Technologies, Saxo Group, Hughes Communications, and UHG — for their invaluable contributions and resources that have deepened my understanding of project management principles.

Lastly, to the readers of this book—thank you for your interest and trust. It is my hope that the insights shared here will empower you to achieve success in your own project management endeavors.

With deepest gratitude,
Puneet Sehgal

Prologue

In every corner of the business world, from multinational corporations to entrepreneurial startups, the ability to effectively manage projects has become not just a desirable skill, but a critical competency for success. As organizations strive to innovate, adapt to change, and deliver value to stakeholders, the role of project management has never been more pivotal.

This book is a culmination of my journey through the intricacies of project management—a discipline that blends art and science, strategy and execution. With over 18 years of experience as a program and project manager, I have witnessed firsthand the impact that well-executed projects can have on an organization's bottom line and its people.

Throughout these pages, I aim to demystify project management fundamentals and equip you with practical tools and strategies that you can apply in your own projects. **Whether you are stepping into a project management role for the first time or seeking to enhance your skills**, this book is designed to serve as a comprehensive guide, covering everything from project initiation and planning to execution, monitoring, and closure.

I invite you to embark on this journey with me—to explore the principles, methodologies, and best practices that underpin successful project management. Together, let's discover how mastering these fundamentals can empower you to lead with confidence, navigate challenges effectively, and drive meaningful outcomes.

As we delve into the world of project management, remember that every project represents an opportunity for growth and innovation. I encourage you to approach each chapter with curiosity and a readiness to apply these insights in your own professional endeavors.

Let's begin our exploration of project management basics, where theory meets practice and where every project holds the promise of transformation.

Puneet Sehgal

Project Management - Introduction and Basics

1. Project Management - Introduction and Basics

Project management is the structured process of leading a team to achieve specific goals and meet specific success criteria within a set timeframe. It involves planning, initiating, executing, monitoring, and closing projects. Effective project management ensures that projects are completed on time, within budget, and to the required quality standards.

2. What is Project Management?

At its core, project management is about organizing resources and guiding teams to achieve defined objectives. A project is a temporary endeavor designed to produce a unique product, service, or result. Unlike ongoing operations, which are repetitive and permanent, projects have a defined beginning and end. This temporary nature means that projects require a tailored approach to planning and execution.

3. Key Elements of Project Management

3.1 **Scope**: The scope defines what the project will deliver. It includes all the work required to complete the project successfully and excludes any work that is not necessary. Clearly defining the scope is crucial to prevent scope creep, where additional tasks and requirements are added without corresponding adjustments to time, cost, or resources.

3.2. **Time**: Time management involves planning the schedule for the project and ensuring that tasks are completed within the agreed-upon timeline. This includes defining activities, sequencing them, estimating the duration, and developing and controlling the schedule.

3.3. **Cost**: Cost management involves estimating, budgeting, and controlling costs so that the project can be completed within the approved budget. This requires careful planning and ongoing monitoring to manage expenses and avoid cost overruns.

3.4. **Quality**: Quality management ensures that the project's deliverables meet the required standards and satisfy the stakeholders. It involves quality planning, quality assurance, and quality control activities.

3.5. **Human Resources**: This element focuses on organizing, managing, and leading the project team. Effective human resource management ensures that the team has the right skills and is motivated to perform at their best.

3.6. **Communication**: Effective communication is vital to project success. It involves planning, managing, and monitoring communications to ensure that all stakeholders are adequately informed and engaged.

3.7. **Risk**: Risk management involves identifying, assessing, and controlling risks that could impact the project's success. It requires proactive planning and continuous monitoring to mitigate potential threats.

3.8. **Procurement**: This involves acquiring goods and services from external sources. Procurement management includes planning, conducting, controlling, and closing procurements.

3.9. **Stakeholder Management**: This element focuses on identifying all stakeholders, understanding their needs and expectations, and engaging them appropriately throughout the project lifecycle.

4. The Project Management Process

The project management process is typically divided into five phases:

4.1. **Initiation**: This phase involves defining the project at a high level. Key activities include developing a project charter, identifying stakeholders, and setting initial objectives and constraints.

4.2. **Planning**: Detailed planning is essential for project success. This phase involves developing a comprehensive project management plan, which includes scope, schedule, cost, quality, resource, communication, risk, and procurement plans. The goal is to create a roadmap that guides the team and provides a baseline for performance measurement.

4.3. **Execution**: During this phase, the project plan is put into action. The focus is on coordinating people and resources, managing stakeholder expectations, and ensuring that project activities are completed as planned. Effective execution requires strong leadership, communication, and problem-solving skills.

4.4. **Monitoring and Controlling**: This phase runs concurrently with execution. It involves tracking project performance, comparing it with the plan, and making adjustments as needed to keep the project on track. Key activities include performance measurement, change control, and risk management.

4.5. **Closing**: The final phase involves formally completing the project. This includes finalizing all activities, obtaining stakeholder approval, and documenting lessons learned. The goal is to ensure that the project deliverables meet the required standards and that the project is officially closed.

5. The Importance of Project Management

Effective project management is crucial for several reasons:

5.1. **Achieving Goals**: It ensures that projects align with organizational goals and deliver the intended outcomes.

5.2. **Resource Optimization**: By planning and managing resources effectively, project management helps optimize the use of time, money, and human resources.

5.3. **Risk Mitigation**: Proactive risk management helps identify potential issues early and develop strategies to mitigate them, reducing the likelihood of project failure.

5.4. **Stakeholder Satisfaction**: By engaging stakeholders and managing their expectations, project management enhances satisfaction and support for the project.

5.5. **Continuous Improvement**: Lessons learned from each project contribute to improved processes and practices, enhancing the organization's ability to deliver successful projects in the future.

6. Conclusion

Project management is a dynamic and multifaceted discipline that plays a critical role in the success of organizations across various industries. By understanding and applying the basics of project management, individuals and teams can effectively navigate the complexities of their projects, achieve their objectives, and deliver value to their stakeholders. As we delve deeper into the specifics of project management methodologies and practices in the subsequent chapters, you will gain the knowledge and skills needed to manage your projects with confidence and efficiency.

ONE
INTRODUCTION TO PROJECT MANAGEMENT

1.1. What is a Project?

In the ever-evolving landscape of business and organizational endeavours, the term "project" has become increasingly prevalent. But what exactly constitutes a project? At its core, a project is a **temporary endeavour undertaken to create a unique product, service, or result**. This definition, while concise, encompasses several key characteristics that distinguish projects from other types of work.

Firstly, the temporary nature of projects is crucial. Every project has a defined beginning and end. This doesn't necessarily mean short-lived; projects can span several years, but they are not ongoing operations. The end of a project is reached when its objectives have been achieved, or when it becomes clear that the objectives cannot be met, or when the need for the project no longer exists.

Secondly, projects result in something unique. This uniqueness can manifest in various ways:

- A product that can be either a component of another item, an enhancement of an item, or an end item in itself
  - A service or the capability to perform a service
  - An improvement in existing product or service lines
  - A result, such as an outcome or document

Examples of projects span across various industries and can include:

- Developing a new pharmaceutical drug
- Constructing a building or bridge
- Implementing a new computer system in an organization
- Launching a marketing campaign
- Planning and executing a community event

It's important to distinguish projects from ongoing operations. While operations are continuous and repetitive, producing the same product or providing the same service over and over, projects are unique and temporary. For instance, manufacturing cars on an assembly line is an ongoing operation, but designing and launching a new car model is a project.

Projects are further characterized by:
- Defined objectives: Clear goals and deliverables that need to be achieved
- Constraints: Limitations typically in terms of time, budget, and scope
- Uncertainty and risk: Due to their unique nature, projects involve a degree of uncertainty and risk

Understanding these characteristics is crucial for effective project management, as they shape the strategies and techniques used to successfully complete projects.

1.2. What is Project Management?

Project management is the **application of knowledge, skills, tools, and techniques to project activities to meet project requirements**. It's a strategic competency for organizations, enabling them to tie project results to business goals — and thus, better compete in their markets.

The value of project management in organizations cannot be overstated. It brings numerous benefits:

1. Improved efficiency and effectiveness: By applying proven project management principles, organizations can execute projects more efficiently, reducing waste of time and resources.

2. Better alignment with business strategy: Project management ensures that the projects undertaken are in line with the organization's overall strategy and goals.

3. Enhanced stakeholder satisfaction: Effective project management leads to better management of stakeholder expectations and improved communication.

4. Risk mitigation: Project management includes processes for identifying, analysing, and responding to project risks, reducing the likelihood of project failure.

5. Improved quality: By focusing on planning and control, project management helps ensure that the project delivers the required quality.

6. Cost savings: Better planning and control often result in cost savings over the life of the project.

Project management involves **five key process groups**:

1. **Initiating**: Defining a new project or a new phase of an existing project by obtaining authorization to start the project or phase.

2. **Planning**: Establishing the scope of the project, refining the objectives, and defining the course of action required to attain the objectives that the project was undertaken to achieve.

3. **Executing**: Completing the work defined in the project management plan to satisfy the project specifications.

4. **Monitoring and Controlling**: Tracking, reviewing, and regulating the progress and performance of the project; identifying any areas in which changes to the plan are required; and initiating the corresponding changes.

5. **Closing**: Formally completing or closing the project or phase.

These process groups are not necessarily sequential and can overlap depending on the project's nature and management approach.

As organizations increasingly recognize the importance of project management, it has evolved into a strategic competency. Many organizations now have Project Management Offices (PMOs) that standardize project-related governance processes and facilitate the sharing of resources, methodologies, tools, and techniques across the organization.

1.3. **The Project Management Triangle**

The Project Management Triangle, also known as the **Triple Constraint** or the Iron Triangle, is a model of the constraints of project management. It contends that the quality of work is constrained by the project's budget, deadlines, and scope. The triangle illustrates the relationship between these three constraints and how changes to one constraint affect the others.

The three constraints are:

1. **Scope**: This refers to what must be done to produce the project's end result. It encompasses all the work involved in creating the products of the project and the processes used to create them. The scope defines the boundaries of the project, determining what will and will not be included.

Scope creep is a common challenge in project management. It refers to uncontrolled changes or continuous growth in a project's scope. This can occur when the project's scope is not properly defined, documented, or controlled. Scope creep can lead to cost overruns, delays, and even project failure.

2. **Time**: This constraint relates to the amount of time available to complete a project. It involves creating a project schedule and ensuring all project tasks are completed within the allocated timeframe.

Effective time management in projects involves:
- Breaking down the project into manageable tasks
- Estimating the duration of each task
- Sequencing the tasks
- Creating a project schedule
- Monitoring progress and making adjustments as necessary

3. **Cost**: This refers to the budgeted amount available for the project. It includes all financial resources needed to complete the project, including labor costs, material costs, equipment costs, and any other expenses.

Cost management involves:
- Estimating costs for each project activity
- Determining the project budget
- Controlling costs throughout the project lifecycle
- Using techniques like Earned Value Management to monitor project performance

At the **centre of the triangle is Quality**. Quality is affected by balancing the three constraints. For example, increasing the scope of the project while maintaining the original budget and schedule could potentially lead to a decrease in quality. Conversely, to increase quality, you might need to increase the budget, extend the schedule, or reduce the scope.

The concept of trade-offs is crucial in understanding the Project Management Triangle. If one constraint is restricted or extended, the other constraints will need to be adjusted accordingly to compensate. For instance:
- If the scope increases, more time and/or money will be needed to deliver the additional requirements.
- If the schedule is shortened, more money may be needed to add resources, or the scope may need to be reduced.
- If the budget is cut, more time might be needed to finish the project with fewer resources, or the scope may need to be reduced.

Understanding and managing these trade-offs is a key skill for project managers. It involves constant communication with stakeholders to manage expectations and make informed decisions about project priorities.

1.4. The Role of a Project Manager

The project manager plays a crucial role in the success of any project. They are responsible for the overall planning, execution, monitoring, control, and closure of a project. Their role is multifaceted, requiring a blend of technical, interpersonal, and business skills.

Key responsibilities of a project manager include:

1. Planning and defining scope: The project manager works with stakeholders to define the project's objectives and deliverables. They create a detailed project plan that outlines the tasks, timelines, and resources required.

2. Resource allocation: This involves identifying and assigning the human, financial, and material resources needed for the project. The project manager must ensure that resources are used effectively and efficiently throughout the project lifecycle.

3. Time and cost management: The project manager is responsible for developing and maintaining the project schedule and budget. They must monitor progress, identify potential delays or cost overruns, and take corrective action when necessary.

4. Risk management: Identifying potential risks, assessing their impact, and developing mitigation strategies is a crucial part of the project manager's role. They must continuously monitor risks throughout the project and adjust plans as needed.

5. Stakeholder communication: The project manager serves as the primary point of contact for all stakeholders. They must ensure clear and consistent communication, manage expectations, and resolve conflicts when they arise.

6. Team leadership: Project managers must lead and motivate their team, fostering a positive work environment and ensuring team members have the support and resources they need to perform their roles effectively.

To fulfil these responsibilities effectively, project managers need a diverse set of skills and competencies:

1. Technical project management skills: These include proficiency in project management methodologies, tools, and techniques. Knowledge of scheduling software, risk management techniques, and financial management are all important.

2. Leadership skills: Project managers must be able to inspire and motivate their team, make decisions, resolve conflicts, and lead by example. They need strong emotional intelligence to navigate the complex interpersonal dynamics often present in project environments.

3. Strategic and business management skills: Understanding how projects align with organizational goals and strategy is crucial. Project managers need business acumen to make decisions that benefit not just the project, but the organization as a whole.

4. Communication skills: Clear, effective communication is perhaps the most important skill for a project manager. They must be able to convey complex information to diverse stakeholders, listen actively, and facilitate productive discussions.

5. Problem-solving skills: Projects often face unexpected challenges. Project managers need to be adept at analysing problems, generating solutions, and making decisions under pressure.

The role of project managers in organizations has been evolving. Increasingly, they are seen not just as technical experts, but as strategic partners who can drive business value. Many organizations now view project management as a career path to senior leadership positions.

Ethical considerations are also a crucial aspect of the project manager's role. They must ensure that the project is conducted in an ethical manner, adhering to legal requirements, organizational policies, and professional standards. This includes considerations such as:
- Honesty and transparency in reporting project status and issues
- Fair treatment of team members and stakeholders
- Responsible use of resources
- Respect for cultural differences in global projects
- Maintaining confidentiality when required
- Avoiding conflicts of interest

By understanding and embracing these responsibilities, skills, and ethical considerations, project managers can effectively lead their projects to success while contributing significant value to their organizations.

1.5. Project Lifecycle Overview

The project lifecycle provides a framework for managing projects. It describes the series of phases that a project passes through from its initiation to its closure. Understanding the project lifecycle is crucial for effective project management as it provides a structure for planning, executing, and controlling project activities.

The typical project lifecycle consists of five phases:

1. **Initiation**

The initiation phase marks the beginning of the project. Its primary purpose is to define the project at a broad level. Key activities in this phase include:

- Defining project goals and objectives: This involves clearly articulating what the project aims to achieve.

- Conducting feasibility studies: These assess whether the project is viable from technical, financial, and operational perspectives.

- Developing the business case: This document justifies the need for the project, outlining its benefits, costs, and risks.

- Identifying key stakeholders: Determining who will be affected by or can influence the project.

- Appointing the project manager and core team members.

- Creating the project charter: This formal document authorizes the project and provides the project manager with the authority to apply organizational resources to project activities.

2. **Planning**

The planning phase is where the project is mapped out in detail. This phase is critical as it sets the foundation for the entire project. Key activities include:

- Developing the project management plan: This comprehensive document outlines how the project will be executed, monitored, and controlled.

- Creating the work breakdown structure (WBS): This hierarchical decomposition of the project scope helps in organizing and defining the total work scope of the project.

- Estimating resources and durations for activities.

- Developing the project schedule and budget.

- Planning for quality management, risk management, and procurement.

- Defining roles and responsibilities within the project team.

3. **Execution**

The execution phase is where the project plan is put into action. This is typically the longest phase of the project lifecycle. Key activities include:

- Coordinating people and resources: Ensuring that the right people are working on the right tasks at the right time.

- Performing the activities defined in the project management plan.

- Implementing the planned methods and standards.

- Creating project deliverables.

- Managing stakeholder expectations: Keeping stakeholders informed and managing their engagement with the project.

- Updating project documentation as changes occur.

4. **Monitoring and Control**

This phase runs concurrently with the execution phase. Its purpose is to measure project progression and performance and to ensure that everything happens according to plan. Key activities include:

- Tracking project performance: Comparing actual performance to planned performance.
- Monitoring and controlling risks.
- Ensuring quality standards are met.
- Managing changes to the project scope, schedule, and budget.
- Taking corrective action when necessary to keep the project on track.
- Providing status reports to stakeholders.

5. **Closure**

The closure phase marks the formal ending of the project. Its purpose is to bring the project to an orderly end. Key activities include:

- Obtaining formal acceptance of deliverables from the client or sponsor.
- Conducting a post-project review to capture lessons learned.
- Closing out all contracts and resolving any outstanding items.
- Releasing project resources.
- Archiving project documents and information.
- Celebrating project completion and recognizing team contributions.

It's important to note that these phases are not always sequential and can overlap. For example, planning often continues into the execution phase as plans are refined based on new information. Similarly, monitoring and control occur throughout the project lifecycle.

Understanding this lifecycle helps project managers and team members anticipate what's coming next in the project, allowing for better planning and management. It provides a structured approach to moving a project from an idea to a finished product or service, ensuring that all necessary steps are taken along the way.

1.6 Core Project Management Knowledge Areas (as defined by PMI)

1. **Integration Management**

Project Integration Management involves coordinating all aspects of a project to ensure that it works as a unified whole. It includes the processes and activities needed to identify, define, combine, unify, and coordinate various processes and project management activities. Key tasks include developing the project charter, creating a project management plan, directing and managing project work, monitoring and controlling project work, performing integrated change control, and closing the project or phase.

2. Scope Management

Project Scope Management ensures that all the work required (and only the work required) is included in the project. This involves defining and controlling what is included in the project. Key processes include planning scope management, collecting requirements, defining scope, creating the Work Breakdown Structure (WBS), validating scope, and controlling scope.

3. Schedule Management

Project Schedule Management involves processes required to manage the timely completion of the project. It includes planning schedule management, defining activities, sequencing activities, estimating activity durations, developing the project schedule, and controlling the schedule. Effective schedule management ensures that the project is completed within the approved timeframe.

4. Cost Management

Project Cost Management encompasses the processes involved in planning, estimating, budgeting, financing, funding, managing, and controlling costs so that the project can be completed within the approved budget. Key processes include planning cost management, estimating costs, determining the budget, and controlling costs.

5. Quality Management

Project Quality Management ensures that the project will satisfy the needs for which it was undertaken. It involves the processes and activities that determine quality policies, objectives, and responsibilities so that the project will meet the needs of stakeholders. Key processes include planning quality management, managing quality, and controlling quality.

6. Resource Management

Project Resource Management involves identifying, acquiring, and managing the resources needed for the successful completion of the project. This includes human resources as well as physical resources. Key processes include planning resource management, estimating resource needs, acquiring resources, developing the team, managing the team, and controlling resources.

7. Communications Management

Project Communications Management ensures timely and appropriate planning, collection, creation, distribution, storage, retrieval, management, control, monitoring, and the ultimate disposition of project information. Key processes include planning communications management, managing communications, and monitoring communications.

8. Risk Management

Project Risk Management involves identifying, analysing, and responding to project risks. It includes maximizing the probability and consequences of positive events and minimizing the probability and consequences of adverse events to project objectives. Key processes include planning risk management, identifying risks, performing qualitative and quantitative risk analysis, planning risk responses, implementing risk responses, and monitoring risks.

9. Procurement Management

Project Procurement Management involves acquiring goods and services from outside the performing organization. It includes the processes necessary to purchase or acquire products, services, or results needed from outside the project team. Key processes include planning procurement management, conducting procurements, controlling procurements, and closing procurements.

10. Stakeholder Management

Project Stakeholder Management involves identifying all people or organizations impacted by the project, analysing stakeholder expectations and their impact on the project, and developing appropriate management strategies for effectively engaging stakeholders in project decisions and execution. Key processes include identifying stakeholders, planning stakeholder engagement, managing stakeholder engagement, and monitoring stakeholder engagement.

1.7 Project Management Methodologies

1. Traditional (Waterfall)

Waterfall is a linear and sequential project management methodology. It consists of distinct phases: requirements, design, implementation, testing, deployment, and maintenance. Each phase must be completed before the next begins, making it easy to manage and track progress. Waterfall is best suited for projects with well-defined requirements and where changes are minimal once the project has started.

2. Agile (Scrum, Kanban)

Agile is an iterative and incremental approach to project management that focuses on flexibility, collaboration, and customer satisfaction.

Scrum: Scrum divides the project into small, manageable pieces called sprints, typically lasting 2-4 weeks. Each sprint ends with a review and retrospective, allowing the team to adapt and improve continuously. Key roles in Scrum include the Product Owner, Scrum Master, and Development Team.

Kanban: Kanban visualizes the workflow using a Kanban board, where tasks are represented as cards that move through various stages of completion. It emphasizes continuous delivery, limiting work in progress, and optimizing flow by identifying and addressing bottlenecks.

3. PRINCE2

PRINCE2 (Projects IN Controlled Environments) is a process-based project management methodology widely used in the UK and internationally. It emphasizes dividing projects into manageable and controllable stages. PRINCE2 is highly structured and includes defined roles, responsibilities, and processes for project management. It is scalable and can be tailored to suit the specific needs of different projects.

4. Six Sigma

Six Sigma is a data-driven methodology focused on improving the quality of process outputs by identifying and removing causes of defects and minimizing variability. It uses a set of quality management tools and follows two key methodologies: DMAIC (Define, Measure, Analyse, Improve, Control) for existing processes and DMADV (Define, Measure, Analyse, Design, Verify) for new processes. Six Sigma aims to achieve near-perfect quality and is often used in manufacturing and production industries.

5. Lean

Lean methodology aims to maximize value by minimizing waste. It focuses on creating more value for customers with fewer resources. Lean principles include identifying value, mapping the value stream, creating flow, establishing pull, and seeking perfection. It emphasizes continuous improvement (Kaizen) and is commonly used in manufacturing, but its principles can be applied to any industry.

6. Hybrid Approaches

Hybrid approaches combine elements from different project management methodologies to create a customized approach that suits the specific needs of a project or organization. For example, a project might use Waterfall for initial planning and Agile for development and execution. Hybrid methodologies aim to leverage the strengths of multiple approaches to address the unique challenges and requirements of each project. They provide flexibility and adaptability, making them suitable for complex and dynamic environments.

1.8. Project Management Office (PMO)

A Project Management Office (PMO) is a management structure that standardizes the project-related governance processes and facilitates the sharing of resources, methodologies, tools, and techniques across an organization. As project management has become increasingly important in organizations, many have established PMOs to improve project success rates and align projects with organizational strategies.

The primary purposes and functions of a PMO include:

1. Standardizing project management practices: PMOs develop and maintain project management standards and methodologies across the organization. This includes creating templates, establishing best practices, and defining project management processes.

2. Facilitating project portfolio management: PMOs often play a key role in selecting and prioritizing projects that align with organizational strategy. They may be involved in business case review, project selection, and resource allocation across multiple projects.

3. Providing training and support to project managers: PMOs often serve as centres of excellence for project management, offering training, mentoring, and support to project managers throughout the organization.

4. Monitoring and reporting on project performance: PMOs typically establish metrics for project success and create dashboards or reports to provide visibility into project and portfolio performance.

5. Managing shared resources across projects: In some organizations, PMOs are responsible for allocating and managing shared project resources.

6. Identifying and developing project management methodology, best practices, and standards.

7. Coaching, mentoring, training and oversight.

8. Monitoring compliance with project management standards, policies, procedures and templates.

9. Developing and managing project policies, procedures, templates and other shared documentation.

10. Coordination between projects.

There are generally **three types of PMOs**, categorized by the degree of control and influence they have on projects within the organization:

1. **Supportive PMO**: This type of PMO provides a consultative role to projects by supplying templates, best practices, training, access to information and lessons learned from other projects. This type of PMO serves as a project repository. The degree of control provided by the PMO is low.

2. **Controlling PMO**: This type of PMO provides support and requires compliance through various means. Compliance may involve adopting specific project management frameworks or methodologies, using specific templates, forms and tools, or conformance to governance. The degree of control provided by the PMO is moderate.

3. **Directive PMO**: This type of PMO takes control of the projects by directly managing the projects. Project managers are assigned by and report to the PMO. The degree of control provided by the PMO is high.

The type of PMO an organization implements depends on its specific needs, culture, and project management maturity level. Some organizations may start with a supportive PMO and evolve towards a more controlling or directive model as their project management practices mature.

It's worth noting that while PMOs can bring significant benefits, they also face challenges. These can include resistance from project managers who feel their autonomy is threatened, difficulty in demonstrating value to senior management, and the risk of becoming overly bureaucratic. Successful PMOs need to balance standardization with flexibility, and control with support, to add value to their organizations.

In conclusion, PMOs play a vital role in many organizations, helping to improve project success rates, standardize practices, and align projects with organizational strategy. Understanding the role and types of PMOs is important for anyone involved in project management, as it provides context for how project management is practiced at an organizational level.

This comprehensive content covers all key aspects of the introduction to project management, providing a solid foundation for the rest of the book.

TWO
PROJECT LIFECYCLE

2.1 Overview of the Project Lifecycle

The project lifecycle is a series of phases that a project goes through from its inception to its completion. Understanding these phases is crucial for effective project management. The five main phases are:
1. Initiation
2. Planning
3. Execution
4. Monitoring and Control
5. Closing
Each phase has specific objectives and deliverables, and they often overlap in practice.

2.2 Initiation Phase

The initiation phase marks the beginning of a project. Key activities include:
- Identifying the project need or opportunity
- Defining project goals and objectives
- Conducting feasibility studies
- Developing the project charter
- Identifying key stakeholders
- Appointing the project manager

Deliverables:
- Project Charter: A document that formally authorizes the project and outlines high-level information about the project.
- Stakeholder Register: A list of all stakeholders, their roles, and their

interests in the project.

2.3 Planning Phase

The planning phase is where the project roadmap is created. Activities include:
- Defining project scope
- Creating the Work Breakdown Structure (WBS)
- Estimating time, cost, and resources
- Developing the project schedule
- Identifying risks and planning responses
- Creating a communication plan
- Developing the project management plan

Deliverables:
- Project Management Plan: A comprehensive document that outlines how the project will be executed, monitored, and controlled.
- Project Schedule: A timeline of project activities and milestones.
- Budget: A detailed estimation of project costs.

2.4 Execution Phase

This is where the actual work of the project is carried out. Key activities include:
- Assembling and developing the project team
- Assigning resources to tasks
- Executing project management plans
- Implementing quality assurance measures
- Managing stakeholder expectations
- Producing project deliverables

Deliverables:
- Project deliverables: The actual products or services that the project was undertaken to create.
- Performance reports: Regular updates on project progress.

2.5 Monitoring and Control Phase

This phase runs concurrently with the execution phase. It involves:
- Tracking project performance
- Comparing actual performance to planned performance

- Identifying variances from the project management plan
- Implementing corrective actions when necessary
- Managing changes to the project scope, schedule, or budget
- Monitoring risks

Deliverables:
- Performance measurements
- Change requests
- Updated project documents

2.6 Closing Phase

The closing phase marks the formal completion of the project. Activities include:
- Obtaining final acceptance of deliverables from stakeholders
- Completing final performance reporting
- Documenting lessons learned
- Archiving project documents
- Releasing project resources
- Conducting post-project review

Deliverables:
- Final product, service, or result
- Formal project closure document
- Lessons learned document

2.7 Iterative and Adaptive Lifecycles

While the traditional lifecycle is linear, many projects, especially in software development, use iterative or adaptive approaches:
- Iterative: The project goes through multiple cycles of planning, execution, and evaluation, refining the product with each iteration.
- Adaptive (Agile): The project evolves through rapid cycles (sprints) of development, testing, and adaptation.
These approaches allow for greater flexibility and responsiveness to changes in project requirements or environment.

2.8 The Importance of Project Lifecycle Management

Understanding and effectively managing the project lifecycle is crucial because it:

- Provides a structured approach to project execution
- Helps in setting clear expectations and milestones
- Facilitates better resource allocation
- Improves risk management
- Enhances stakeholder communication
- Increases the likelihood of project success

Conclusion:

The project lifecycle provides a framework for managing projects from start to finish. By understanding and effectively navigating each phase, project managers can ensure that their projects are well-organized, efficiently executed, and successfully completed. In the following chapters, we will delve deeper into the specific knowledge areas and skills required to manage each phase of the project lifecycle effectively.

THREE

PROJECT INITIATION

3.1. Identifying Business Needs and Opportunities

The project initiation phase begins with recognizing a business need or opportunity that could be addressed through a project. This crucial step sets the foundation for the entire project and determines whether it aligns with the organization's strategic objectives.

Analysing Market Trends and Organizational Goals:

To identify relevant business needs and opportunities, organizations must:

1. Conduct market research: This involves analysing current market conditions, customer needs, and competitor activities. Tools like PESTLE analysis (Political, Economic, Social, Technological, Legal, and Environmental factors) can provide valuable insights.

2. Review organizational strategy: Projects should align with the organization's mission, vision, and strategic objectives. This ensures that resources are allocated to initiatives that contribute to the company's long-term goals.

3. Identify performance gaps: Compare the organization's current performance with desired performance levels to pinpoint areas for improvement.

4. Gather stakeholder input: Consult with key stakeholders, including customers, employees, and management, to identify pain points and potential opportunities.

5. Analyse industry trends: Stay informed about emerging technologies, changing regulations, and shifts in consumer behaviour that could impact the business.

Conducting Feasibility Studies:

Once potential project ideas are identified, feasibility studies help determine whether they are viable. A comprehensive feasibility study typically includes:

1. Technical feasibility: Assesses whether the organization has the necessary technology and expertise to execute the project.

2. Economic feasibility: Evaluates the project's potential return on investment (ROI) and financial viability.

3. Legal feasibility: Examines any legal or regulatory constraints that might impact the project.

4. Operational feasibility: Determines whether the organization has the operational capacity to undertake and benefit from the project.

5. Schedule feasibility: Assesses whether the project can be completed within a reasonable timeframe.

The outcome of these analyses forms the basis for deciding whether to proceed with the project.

3.2. Developing the Project Charter

The project charter is a critical document that formally authorizes the existence of the project and provides the project manager with the authority to apply organizational resources to project activities.

Purpose and Components of a Project Charter:

The project charter serves several key purposes:

1. Formally recognizes the existence of the project

2. Provides a high-level description of the project and its boundaries

3. Establishes the project manager's authority

4. Secures management commitment to the project

A comprehensive project charter typically includes:

1. Project Purpose or Justification: A clear statement of why the project is being undertaken.

2. Measurable Project Objectives: Specific, measurable goals that the project aims to achieve.

3. High-level Requirements: A summary of the key deliverables or features of the project.

4. High-level Project Description: An overview of the project's scope and key deliverables.

5. High-level Risks: Initial identification of known risks that could impact the project.

6. Summary Milestone Schedule: Key project milestones and their estimated completion dates.

7. Summary Budget: A high-level budget or cost estimate for the project.

8. Project Approval Requirements: Criteria that will be used to judge project success.

9. Assigned Project Manager and Authority Level: Name of the project manager and their level of authority.

10. Name and Authority of the Sponsor: The individual or group sponsoring and championing the project.

Writing an Effective Project Charter:

To create an effective project charter:

1. Be concise: The charter should be brief yet comprehensive, typically 3-5 pages.

2. Use clear language: Avoid jargon and technical terms that may not be understood by all stakeholders.

3. Be specific: Provide concrete details where possible, especially for objectives and success criteria.

4. Involve key stakeholders: Ensure that all relevant parties have input into the charter's development.

5. Align with organizational goals: Clearly demonstrate how the project supports the organization's strategic objectives.

Getting Stakeholder Approval:

Obtaining approval for the project charter is a critical step. This typically involves:

1. Presenting the charter to key stakeholders, including the project sponsor and senior management.

2. Addressing any questions or concerns raised by stakeholders.

3. Making necessary revisions based on stakeholder feedback.

4. Obtaining formal sign-off from the project sponsor and other required parties.

5. Distributing the approved charter to all relevant stakeholders.

3.3. Stakeholder Identification and Analysis

Stakeholder management is crucial for project success. It begins with identifying who the stakeholders are and understanding their potential impact on the project.

Identifying Key Stakeholders:

Stakeholders are individuals, groups, or organizations that may affect, be affected by, or perceive themselves to be affected by a decision, activity, or outcome of the project. Key stakeholders often include:

1. Project sponsor

2. Customers or end-users

3. Project team members

4. Functional managers

5. Senior management

6. Suppliers or vendors

7. Regulatory bodies

8. Competitors

9. Community groups or the general public

To identify stakeholders:

1. Brainstorm with the project team and sponsor

2. Review organizational charts and process flows

3. Examine past project stakeholder lists

4. Consider external entities that might be impacted by the project

Stakeholder Mapping Techniques:

Once stakeholders are identified, they need to be analysed to understand their potential impact on the project. Common stakeholder mapping techniques include:

1. Power/Interest Grid: This technique plots stakeholders on a matrix based on their level of power (ability to influence the project) and interest (level of concern about the project outcomes).

Power/Interest Grid

2. Salience Model: This model categorizes stakeholders based on their power, legitimacy, and urgency.

Power: Ability to influence the project

Legitimacy: Appropriate involvement in the project

Urgency: Need for immediate attention

3. Stakeholder Engagement Assessment Matrix: This tool helps in understanding current and desired stakeholder engagement levels, such as unaware, resistant, neutral, supportive, or leading.

Understanding Stakeholder Influence and Interest:

After mapping stakeholders, it's crucial to delve deeper into understanding their specific interests, expectations, and potential influence on the project. This involves:

1. Conducting stakeholder interviews or surveys

2. Analysing stakeholder's past behaviour in similar projects

3. Identifying potential conflicts between stakeholders

4. Determining each stakeholder's communication needs and preferences

This analysis forms the basis for developing stakeholder engagement strategies in later project phases.

3.4. Defining Project Objectives and Scope

Clear project objectives and a well-defined scope are essential for project success. They provide direction for the project team and set expectations for stakeholders.

Setting SMART Objectives:

Project objectives should follow the SMART criteria:

Specific: Clearly state what is to be achieved

Measurable: Include metrics to determine if the objective has been met

Achievable: Ensure the objective is realistic given available resources and constraints

Relevant: Align with organizational goals and strategies

Time-bound: Specify when the objective should be achieved

For example, instead of "Improve customer satisfaction," a SMART objective would be "Increase customer satisfaction ratings by 15% within 6 months of project completion, as measured by our quarterly customer survey."

Creating a Preliminary Scope Statement:

The preliminary scope statement provides a high-level description of the project and product scope. It typically includes:

1. Product scope description: The features and functions that characterize the product, service, or result

2. Project deliverables: Tangible and verifiable products, results, or capabilities

3. Project boundaries: What is and is not included in the project

4. Acceptance criteria: Conditions that must be met for deliverables to be accepted

5. Project constraints: Factors that limit the project team's options

6. Project assumptions: Factors assumed to be true for planning purposes

Identifying Project Boundaries and Constraints:

Clearly defining what is and isn't included in the project helps manage stakeholder expectations and prevent scope creep. Key considerations include:

1. Boundaries: Explicit statements of what work is included and excluded from the project

2. Time constraints: Deadlines or time-based limitations

3. Budget constraints: Financial limitations

4. Resource constraints: Limitations on personnel, equipment, or materials

5. Quality constraints: Required standards or regulations

6. Risk tolerance: The level of risk the organization is willing to accept

By thoroughly addressing these aspects of project initiation, organizations can lay a strong foundation for project success, aligning the project with business needs, securing stakeholder support, and setting clear direction for the project team.

This comprehensive content covers the key aspects of project initiation, providing a solid foundation for understanding how projects are conceived and formally started.

FOUR

PROJECT PLANNING

4.1. Developing the Project Management Plan

The project management plan is the central document that defines how the project is executed, monitored, and controlled. It integrates and consolidates all of the subsidiary management plans and baselines from the planning process.

Components of a Comprehensive Project Management Plan:

1. Scope Management Plan: Describes how the project scope will be defined, developed, monitored, controlled, and validated.

2. Requirements Management Plan: Outlines how requirements will be analysed, documented, and managed.

3. Schedule Management Plan: Establishes the criteria and activities for developing, monitoring, and controlling the project schedule.

4. Cost Management Plan: Provides guidance on how project costs will be planned, structured, and controlled.

5. Quality Management Plan: Describes how quality policies will be implemented to ensure project deliverables meet specified requirements.

6. Resource Management Plan: Defines how project resources (team members, equipment, materials) will be acquired, allocated, monitored, and controlled.

7. Communications Management Plan: Describes how, when, and by whom project information will be administered and disseminated.

8. Risk Management Plan: Outlines how risk management activities will be structured and performed.

9. Procurement Management Plan: Describes how the project team will acquire goods and services from outside the performing organization.

10. Stakeholder Engagement Plan: Outlines strategies to effectively engage stakeholders throughout the project lifecycle.

Integrating Subsidiary Plans:

The project manager must ensure that all these subsidiary plans are consistent with each other and with the overall project objectives. This involves:

1. Identifying interdependencies between different plan components

2. Resolving conflicts or inconsistencies between plans

3. Ensuring all plans align with the project charter and objectives

4. Regularly reviewing and updating plans as the project progresses

4.2. Scope Planning

Effective scope planning is crucial for project success. It involves defining and controlling what is and is not included in the project.

Creating the Work Breakdown Structure (WBS):

The WBS is a hierarchical decomposition of the total scope of work to be carried out by the project team. Key steps in creating a WBS include:

1. Identify major deliverables and sub-deliverables

2. Organize these deliverables into a hierarchical structure

3. Decompose higher-level elements into smaller, more manageable components

4. Assign unique identifiers to each WBS element

5. Ensure that the lowest level of decomposition (work package) is sufficient for estimating, scheduling, and controlling

Defining Work Packages:

Work packages are the lowest level in the WBS and represent assignable units of work. Characteristics of well-defined work packages include:

1. Clear scope definition

2. Start and end dates

3. Estimated cost and resource requirements

4. Assignable to a single individual or organization

5. Manageable size (typically 8-80 hours of work)

6. Measurable progress

Scope Baseline and Scope Statement:

The scope baseline includes the approved project scope statement, WBS, and WBS dictionary. The scope statement typically includes:

1. Product scope description

2. Project deliverables

3. Acceptance criteria

4. Project exclusions

5. Constraints and assumptions

The scope baseline serves as a reference point for managing changes and measuring project performance.

4.3. Schedule Planning

Schedule planning involves defining project activities, sequencing them, estimating their durations, and developing the project schedule.

Activity Definition and Sequencing:

1. Identify specific activities that need to be performed to produce project deliverables

2. Document dependencies between activities (e.g., finish-to-start, start-to-start)

3. Determine any lead or lag time between activities

Estimating Activity Durations:

Techniques for estimating durations include:

1. Expert judgment

2. Analogous estimating (based on similar past projects)

3. Parametric estimating (using statistical relationships)

4. Three-point estimating (using optimistic, most likely, and pessimistic estimates)

Critical Path Method:

The critical path is the sequence of activities that represents the longest path through the project, determining the shortest possible project duration. Steps in critical path analysis include:

1. Construct a network diagram of all project activities

2. Estimate the duration for each activity

3. Identify the early start, early finish, late start, and late finish for each activity

4. Calculate total float for each activity

5. Identify the critical path (activities with zero float)

Gantt Charts and Network Diagrams:

Gantt charts provide a bar chart representation of the project schedule, showing start and finish dates of activities and their dependencies. Network diagrams show the logical relationships between activities.

4.4. Cost Planning

Cost planning involves estimating, budgeting, and controlling project costs.

Cost Estimation Techniques:

1. Analogous estimating: Using costs from similar past projects

2. Parametric estimating: Using statistical relationships between historical data and variables

3. Bottom-up estimating: Estimating individual work packages and rolling up

4. Three-point estimating: Using optimistic, most likely, and pessimistic estimates

Developing the Project Budget:

Steps in budget development include:

1. Aggregating estimated costs of individual activities or work packages

2. Adding contingency reserves for known risks

3. Adding management reserves for unknown risks

4. Establishing cost baseline

Cost Baseline:

The cost baseline is the approved version of the time-phased project budget, excluding management reserves. It's used as a basis for measuring and monitoring cost performance.

4.5. Quality Planning

Quality planning involves identifying quality requirements and standards for the project and its deliverables, and documenting how the project will demonstrate compliance.

Defining Quality Standards and Metrics:

1. Identify relevant quality standards (e.g., ISO standards, industry-specific standards)

2. Define quality metrics for project deliverables

3. Establish quality targets and tolerances

Quality Assurance vs. Quality Control:

Quality Assurance (QA) focuses on the processes used to manage and deliver the solution. It involves regular process audits and improvements.

Quality Control (QC) focuses on identifying defects in project deliverables. It involves inspections, testing, and measurements against defined quality standards.

Creating the Quality Management Plan:

The quality management plan describes how quality policies will be implemented. It typically includes:

1. Quality standards to be used

2. Quality objectives

3. Quality assurance activities

4. Quality control activities

5. Quality tools to be used

6. Roles and responsibilities for quality management

4.6. Resource Planning

Resource planning involves identifying and acquiring the resources (people, equipment, materials) needed for successful project completion.

Identifying Required Resources:

1. Review the WBS and activity list to determine resource requirements

2. Consider skill sets needed for each activity

3. Identify equipment and materials needed

Resource Allocation and Levelling:

Resource allocation involves assigning resources to project activities. Resource levelling aims to minimize fluctuations in resource usage over time.

Creating the Resource Management Plan:

The resource management plan outlines:

1. Roles and responsibilities of team members

2. Project organization charts

3. Staff acquisition strategy

4. Resource calendars

5. Training needs

6. Team development approach

4.7. Communications Planning

Effective communication is crucial for project success. Communications planning involves determining the information and communication needs of project stakeholders.

Identifying Communication Needs of Stakeholders:

1. Review stakeholder register and engagement requirements

2. Determine information needs for each stakeholder group

3. Establish frequency and methods of communication

Developing the Communications Management Plan:

The communications management plan outlines:

1. Stakeholder communication requirements

2. Information to be communicated (format, content, level of detail)

3. Frequency of communication

4. Methods or technologies used to convey information

5. Responsible person for each type of communication

6. Escalation process for resolving issues

4.8. Risk Planning

Risk planning involves identifying potential risks, analysing their potential impact, and developing response strategies.

Detailed Risk Identification and Analysis:

1. Use techniques such as brainstorming, SWOT analysis, and reviewing historical data

2. Categorize risks (e.g., technical, external, organizational, project management)

3. Assess probability and impact of each identified risk

4. Prioritize risks based on their overall risk score

Risk Response Strategies:

For negative risks (threats):

1. Avoid: Eliminate the threat by eliminating the cause

2. Transfer: Shift the impact and management to a third party

3. Mitigate: Reduce probability and/or impact

4. Accept: Acknowledge the risk but take no proactive action

For positive risks (opportunities):

1. Exploit: Ensure the opportunity is realized

2. Enhance: Increase the probability and/or impact

3. Share: Allocate ownership to a third party better able to capture the opportunity

4. Accept: Take advantage of the opportunity if it arises, but don't pursue it

Creating the Risk Management Plan:

The risk management plan outlines:

1. Methodology for risk management

2. Roles and responsibilities

3. Budgeting for risk management

4. Timing and frequency of risk management processes

5. Risk categories and definitions

6. Stakeholder risk tolerances

7. Reporting formats and tracking processes

4.9. Procurement Planning

Procurement planning involves determining whether to acquire goods and services from outside the project organization and, if so, what to acquire and how.

Make-or-Buy Decisions:

Analyse whether it's more cost-effective to make an item or perform an activity internally, or to buy it from an external source. Consider factors such as:

1. Core competencies of the organization
2. Capacity and capabilities
3. Cost comparisons
4. Risks associated with each option

Vendor Selection Criteria:

Establish criteria for evaluating potential vendors, such as:

1. Technical capability
2. Management approach
3. Cost competitiveness
4. Past performance
5. Financial stability

Developing the Procurement Management Plan:

The procurement management plan outlines:

1. Types of contracts to be used
2. Risk management issues related to procurement
3. Standardized procurement documents
4. Procurement constraints and assumptions
5. Coordination of procurement with project schedule and performance reporting
6. Metrics for managing procurements

By thoroughly addressing these aspects of project planning, project managers can create a comprehensive roadmap for project execution, setting the stage for successful project delivery.

This comprehensive content covers the key aspects of project planning, providing a detailed guide on how to develop the various components of a project plan.

FIVE

PROJECT EXECUTION

5.1. Directing and Managing Project Work

The execution phase is where the project plan is put into action. The project manager's role during this phase is to coordinate people and resources, as well as integrate and perform the activities of the project in accordance with the project management plan.

Implementing the Project Management Plan:

1. Coordinate planned activities: Ensure that all team members understand their roles and responsibilities.

2. Allocate resources: Assign resources to scheduled tasks based on the resource management plan.

3. Implement planned methods and standards: Follow the processes outlined in the various management plans (quality, communications, risk, etc.).

4. Establish and manage communication channels: Set up regular team meetings, status reports, and other communication methods as per the communications management plan.

Managing Work Packages and Deliverables:

1. Monitor progress of work packages: Track completion of tasks against the project schedule.

2. Review deliverables: Ensure that completed work meets the defined acceptance criteria.

3. Coordinate deliverables: Manage interdependencies between different work packages and deliverables.

4. Document lessons learned: Capture insights and experiences throughout the execution phase to inform future projects.

Addressing Changes and Issues as They Arise:

1. Identify changes and issues: Be vigilant for any deviations from the plan or new risks that emerge.

2. Assess impact: Evaluate how changes or issues affect project scope, schedule, budget, and quality.

3. Implement change control processes: Follow established procedures for reviewing, approving, and implementing changes.

4. Update project documents: Revise project plans and documents to reflect approved changes.

5.2. Quality Assurance and Control

Quality management during project execution involves both quality assurance (focusing on processes) and quality control (focusing on deliverables).

Implementing Quality Assurance Processes:

1. Process analysis: Regularly review project processes to identify areas for improvement.

2. Quality audits: Conduct independent evaluations to determine whether project activities comply with organizational policies, processes, and procedures.

3. Root cause analysis: When issues are identified, perform root cause analysis to address underlying problems rather than just symptoms.

4. Continuous improvement: Implement process improvements based on audit findings and analysis results.

Conducting Quality Control Activities:

1. Inspections: Examine work products to determine if they meet specified standards.

2. Testing: Conduct tests to ensure deliverables meet functional and performance requirements.

3. Statistical sampling: Use appropriate sampling methods to evaluate quality of large quantities of items.

4. Defect tracking: Maintain a log of identified defects, their resolution status, and trends over time.

Using Quality Tools and Techniques:

1. Control charts: Monitor process stability and identify when a process is out of control.

2. Cause-and-effect diagrams: Identify potential causes of quality issues.

3. Histograms: Visualize the frequency distribution of quality data.

4. Pareto charts: Identify the vital few sources of defects to prioritize corrective actions.

5.3. Team Development and Management

Effective team management is crucial for project success. The project manager must focus on building a high-performing team and maintaining team motivation throughout the project.

Building and Motivating the Project Team:

1. Team building activities: Organize events or exercises that promote team cohesion and trust.

2. Clear roles and responsibilities: Ensure each team member understands their role and how it contributes to project success.

3. Recognition and rewards: Acknowledge good performance and milestone achievements.

4. Empowerment: Delegate authority and encourage team members to make decisions within their areas of responsibility.

5. Professional development: Provide opportunities for team members to enhance their skills and knowledge.

Conflict Resolution Strategies:

1. Identify the source of conflict: Understand the root cause of disagreements or issues.

2. Encourage open communication: Create a safe environment for team members to express concerns.

3. Focus on interests, not positions: Help conflicting parties identify underlying needs and interests.

4. Generate multiple solutions: Brainstorm various ways to resolve the conflict.

5. Agree on a resolution: Facilitate agreement on the best solution and document the decision.

6. Follow up: Monitor the implementation of the resolution and its effectiveness.

Performance Management and Feedback:

1. Set clear expectations: Ensure team members understand performance standards and project goals.

2. Regular check-ins: Conduct one-on-one meetings to discuss progress, challenges, and support needed.

3. Constructive feedback: Provide specific, timely, and actionable feedback on performance.

4. Performance evaluations: Conduct formal evaluations as per organizational policy and project needs.

5. Address underperformance: Promptly address performance issues through coaching and support.

5.4. Information Distribution and Communication

Effective communication is vital for keeping all stakeholders informed and engaged throughout the project execution phase.

Implementing the Communications Plan:

1. Follow the communication schedule: Adhere to the frequency and methods outlined in the communications management plan.

2. Tailor communication: Adjust the content and format of information based on stakeholder needs and preferences.

3. Use appropriate channels: Utilize the most effective communication channels for different types of information and stakeholders.

4. Maintain communication logs: Keep records of key communications for future reference and audit purposes.

Conducting Effective Meetings:

1. Prepare and distribute agendas: Clearly outline meeting objectives and topics to be discussed.

2. Invite relevant participants: Ensure the right people are present to make necessary decisions.

3. Facilitate discussions: Keep the meeting focused and encourage participation from all attendees.

4. Document decisions and action items: Record key decisions, assigned tasks, and deadlines.

5. Follow up: Distribute meeting minutes and track completion of action items.

Status Reporting and Documentation:

1. Regular status reports: Provide updates on project progress, issues, risks, and upcoming activities.

2. Dashboard reporting: Use visual representations of key project metrics for easy stakeholder consumption.

3. Milestone reporting: Highlight the achievement of significant project milestones.

4. Issue and risk logs: Maintain up-to-date records of project issues and risks, including their status and mitigation actions.

5. Document repository: Maintain a centralized, organized system for storing and accessing project documents.

5.5. Procurement Management

During project execution, the project manager must oversee the procurement process to ensure that all necessary goods and services are acquired according to the project's needs and specifications.

Conducting Procurements:

1. Prepare procurement documents: Develop detailed specifications, work statements, or terms of reference.

2. Advertise opportunities: If required, publicly announce procurement opportunities.

3. Conduct bidder conferences: Hold meetings to provide additional information to potential sellers and address questions.

4. Evaluate proposals: Use the predetermined evaluation criteria to assess and score vendor proposals.

5. Select vendors: Choose the most suitable vendor(s) based on evaluation results and negotiation outcomes.

6. Award contracts: Formally engage selected vendors through appropriate contractual agreements.

Vendor Management and Contract Administration:

1. Kick-off meetings: Hold initial meetings with vendors to align expectations and review contract terms.

2. Performance monitoring: Regularly assess vendor performance against contract requirements and project needs.

3. Payment processing: Ensure timely processing of vendor invoices in accordance with contract terms.

4. Change management: Handle any changes to contract scope, terms, or conditions through formal change control processes.

5. Issue resolution: Address any conflicts or issues with vendors promptly and professionally.

6. Contract closure: Ensure all contractual obligations are met before formally closing out vendor contracts.

5.6. Stakeholder Engagement

Effective stakeholder management is crucial throughout the project, particularly during the execution phase when the impact of the project becomes more visible.

Managing Stakeholder Expectations:

1. Regular updates: Keep stakeholders informed about project progress, changes, and upcoming activities.

2. Transparency: Be open about challenges and risks, as well as successes.

3. Expectation setting: Continuously align stakeholder expectations with project realities.

4. Feedback collection: Regularly solicit and act on stakeholder feedback.

Implementing Stakeholder Engagement Strategies:

1. Tailor engagement: Use appropriate engagement methods for different stakeholder groups based on their influence and interest.

2. Build relationships: Foster positive relationships through regular interaction and responsiveness.

3. Address concerns: Promptly address stakeholder concerns and demonstrate how their input is considered.

4. Leverage support: Engage supportive stakeholders to influence others and build project momentum.

5. Manage resistance: Identify sources of stakeholder resistance and develop targeted strategies to address concerns.

5.7. Risk Monitoring and Response

Risk management continues throughout the execution phase, with a focus on monitoring identified risks and implementing planned responses.

Implementing Risk Responses:

1. Preventive actions: Implement planned actions to reduce the probability or impact of negative risks.

2. Exploitative actions: Take steps to increase the likelihood of positive risks (opportunities) occurring.

3. Contingency plans: Execute pre-planned responses when risk triggers occur.

4. Workarounds: Develop and implement unplanned responses to emerging risks or issues.

Continuous Risk Monitoring and Reassessment:

1. Regular risk reviews: Conduct periodic reviews of the risk register to assess the status of identified risks.

2. New risk identification: Continuously scan for new risks that may emerge during project execution.

3. Risk response effectiveness: Evaluate the effectiveness of implemented risk responses and adjust as necessary.

4. Risk metric tracking: Monitor key risk indicators to identify trends and potential issues.

5. Risk communication: Keep stakeholders informed about significant risks and their potential impacts.

5.8. Managing Project Changes

Change is inevitable in most projects. Effective change management is crucial to maintain project control and ensure that changes are beneficial to the project.

Change Control Processes:

1. Change request submission: Establish a clear process for stakeholders to submit change requests.

2. Impact assessment: Analyse the potential impact of proposed changes on project scope, schedule, budget, and quality.

3. Change review: Convene the change control board (or equivalent authority) to review and decide on proposed changes.

4. Decision communication: Promptly communicate decisions on change requests to relevant stakeholders.

5. Change implementation: For approved changes, update project plans and execute the changes.

Evaluating and Approving Change Requests:

1. Alignment with project objectives: Assess how the proposed change aligns with overall project goals.

2. Cost-benefit analysis: Evaluate the potential benefits of the change against its costs and risks.

3. Resource availability: Consider whether the project has the necessary resources to implement the change.

4. Timing considerations: Assess the optimal timing for implementing the change within the project timeline.

5. Stakeholder impact: Consider how the change will affect various stakeholder groups.

Updating Project Documents and Plans:

1. Project management plan updates: Revise relevant sections of the project management plan to reflect approved changes.

2. Scope baseline updates: Modify the scope statement, WBS, and WBS dictionary as necessary.

3. Schedule updates: Adjust the project schedule to accommodate changes in activities or timelines.

4. Budget updates: Revise the cost baseline to reflect any financial implications of approved changes.

5. Other document updates: Update risk register, quality management plan, and other relevant project documents.

By effectively managing these aspects of project execution, project managers can ensure that the project progresses as planned, while remaining flexible enough to handle the inevitable challenges and changes that arise during this phase.

This comprehensive content covers the key aspects of project execution, providing a detailed guide on how to implement the project plan and manage the various elements of the project during this critical phase.

SIX

PROJECT MONITORING AND CONTROL

6.1. Overview of Monitoring and Control Processes

Project monitoring and control is a critical phase that runs concurrently with project execution. It involves tracking, reviewing, and regulating the progress and performance of the project to ensure that it meets its objectives.

Purpose and Importance of Monitoring and Control:

1. Performance measurement: Regularly assess project performance against the baseline plan.

2. Variance identification: Detect deviations from the project management plan.

3. Corrective action: Implement changes to bring expected future performance in line with the project management plan.

4. Preventive action: Reduce the probability of negative consequences associated with project risks.

5. Forecasting: Project future status and performance based on current performance and trends.

Key Performance Indicators (KPIs) in Project Management:

KPIs are measurable values that demonstrate how effectively a project is achieving its key objectives. Common project KPIs include:

1. Schedule Performance Index (SPI)

2. Cost Performance Index (CPI)

3. Return on Investment (ROI)

4. Customer Satisfaction Score

5. Defect Frequency

6. Resource Utilization

7. Risk Mitigation Effectiveness

6.2. Monitoring Project Work

Effective monitoring involves systematically collecting and analysing project performance data to ensure the project is on track.

Tracking Progress Against the Project Management Plan:

1. Work performance measurements: Collect data on actual start and finish dates, costs incurred, and percent completion of schedule activities.

2. Variance analysis: Compare actual performance with planned performance to identify deviations.

3. Trend analysis: Examine project performance over time to determine if performance is improving or deteriorating.

Data Collection and Analysis Techniques:

1. Status meetings: Regular team meetings to discuss progress, issues, and upcoming work.

2. Time reporting systems: Tools for team members to log their time spent on project activities.

3. Earned Value Management (EVM): A technique that combines scope, schedule, and resource measurements to assess project performance and progress.

4. Critical path analysis: Monitoring the status of activities on the critical path to ensure project completion on time.

Performance Reporting:

1. Status reports: Regular reports detailing project progress, accomplishments, and upcoming activities.

2. Variance reports: Documents detailing any deviations from the baseline plan, including schedule and cost variances.

3. Forecasts: Predictions of future project status and performance based on current performance data.

4. Progress dashboards: Visual representations of key project metrics and KPIs.

6.3. Integrated Change Control

Integrated change control is the process of reviewing all change requests, approving or rejecting changes, and managing changes to project deliverables, organizational process assets, project documents, and the project management plan.

Managing Change Requests:

1. Change request submission: Establish a formal process for stakeholders to submit change requests.

2. Change log: Maintain a record of all submitted change requests and their status.

3. Initial screening: Perform a preliminary assessment of change requests to determine if they warrant further consideration.

Impact Analysis of Proposed Changes:

1. Scope impact: Assess how the change would affect project deliverables and requirements.

2. Schedule impact: Determine the effect on project timelines and milestones.

3. Cost impact: Evaluate the financial implications of the proposed change.

4. Quality impact: Consider how the change might affect the quality of project deliverables.

5. Risk impact: Identify any new risks or changes to existing risk levels resulting from the proposed change.

6. Resource impact: Assess the effect on resource allocation and utilization.

Change Control Board and Decision-Making Processes:

1. Change Control Board (CCB) composition: Establish a group of stakeholders responsible for reviewing and deciding on change requests.

2. CCB meetings: Regular meetings to review pending change requests.

3. Decision criteria: Develop and apply consistent criteria for evaluating change requests.

4. Documentation: Record decisions, rationales, and any follow-up actions required.

5. Communication: Inform relevant stakeholders of CCB decisions and their implications.

6.4. Scope Verification and Control

Scope verification and control ensure that all requested changes and recommended corrective actions are processed through the integrated change control process.

Validating Deliverables:

1. Inspection: Examine deliverables to determine if they meet project requirements and product specifications.

2. Client acceptance: Obtain formal acceptance of deliverables from the client or sponsor.

3. Quality audits: Conduct independent reviews to ensure deliverables meet quality standards.

Managing Scope Creep:

1. Scope baseline monitoring: Regularly compare current project scope against the approved scope baseline.

2. Change request analysis: Carefully evaluate the impact of proposed scope changes.

3. Scope change communication: Ensure all stakeholders are aware of approved scope changes and their implications.

Updating Scope Documentation:

1. Work performance measurements: Document the status of project deliverables and work performance.

2. Organizational process asset updates: Update any organizational standards or guidelines based on project experiences.

3. Change request updates: Maintain current status of change requests in the change log.

6.5. Schedule Control

Schedule control involves monitoring the status of the project to update project progress and manage changes to the schedule baseline.

Schedule Variance Analysis:

1. Schedule Performance Index (SPI): Calculate SPI to determine if the project is ahead of or behind schedule.

2. Schedule variance: Quantify the difference between planned and actual progress.

3. Trend analysis: Examine schedule performance over time to identify patterns.

Schedule Compression Techniques:

1. Fast tracking: Perform activities in parallel that would normally be done in sequence.

2. Crashing: Add resources to critical path activities to complete them in less time.

Updating the Project Schedule:

1. Status updates: Regularly update activity status, actual start and finish dates, and percent complete.

2. Forecasting: Estimate future schedule performance based on past performance.

3. Schedule narrative: Document explanations for major variances and corrective actions taken.

6.6. Cost Control

Cost control involves monitoring the status of the project to update the project budget and manage changes to the cost baseline.

Earned Value Management (EVM):

EVM is a powerful technique that integrates scope, schedule, and resource measurements for assessing project performance.

Key EVM metrics include:

1. Planned Value (PV): The authorized budget assigned to scheduled work.

2. Earned Value (EV): The value of work actually completed.

3. Actual Cost (AC): The total cost incurred in accomplishing work.

4. Cost Variance (CV): The difference between earned value and actual cost ($CV = EV - AC$).

5. Schedule Variance (SV): The difference between earned value and planned value ($SV = EV - PV$).

6. Cost Performance Index (CPI): The ratio of earned value to actual cost ($CPI = EV / AC$).

7. Schedule Performance Index (SPI): The ratio of earned value to planned value ($SPI = EV / PV$).

Cost Variance Analysis:

1. Identify variances: Compare actual costs to budgeted costs for each work package and control account.

2. Determine causes: Investigate reasons for cost variances, such as estimating errors, scope changes, or productivity issues.

3. Impact assessment: Evaluate how cost variances affect the overall project budget and completion cost.

Forecasting and Updating the Budget:

1. Estimate at Completion (EAC): Forecast the total cost of completing all work based on performance to date.

2. Estimate to Complete (ETC): Estimate the cost of completing remaining work.

3. Budget updates: Revise project budget based on approved changes and current performance data.

4. Funding limit reconciliation: Ensure projected funding needs are reconciled with funding limits.

6.7. Quality Control

Quality control involves monitoring specific project results to determine if they comply with relevant quality standards and identifying ways to eliminate causes of unsatisfactory performance.

Quality Audits and Inspections:

1. Process audits: Review project processes to ensure they are efficient and effective.

2. Product inspections: Examine project deliverables to ensure they meet specified requirements.

3. Defect tracking: Maintain a log of identified defects, their status, and resolution.

Statistical Sampling:

1. Sample selection: Choose a representative subset of deliverables for inspection.

2. Acceptance criteria: Establish clear criteria for accepting or rejecting the sampled items.

3. Analysis and reporting: Analyse sampling results and report findings to relevant stakeholders.

Continuous Improvement Processes:

1. Lessons learned: Regularly capture insights and best practices throughout the project.

2. Process analysis: Identify inefficiencies or bottlenecks in project processes.

3. Corrective action: Implement improvements to address identified quality issues.

4. Preventive action: Take steps to prevent potential quality problems from occurring.

6.8. Performance Reporting

Performance reporting involves collecting and distributing performance information, including status reports, progress measurements, and forecasts.

Creating Effective Project Status Reports:

1. Executive summary: Provide a high-level overview of project status, key achievements, and major issues.

2. Schedule status: Report on progress against key milestones and overall schedule performance.

3. Budget status: Present cost performance data and any significant variances.

4. Scope status: Update on deliverables completed and any scope changes.

5. Risk and issue summary: Highlight key risks and issues, along with mitigation strategies.

6. Next steps: Outline upcoming activities and key decisions needed.

Dashboards and Visual Reporting Techniques:

1. Key Performance Indicator (KPI) dashboards: Visual displays of critical project metrics.

2. Burndown charts: Graphical representation of work left to do versus time.

3. Milestone trend charts: Visual tracking of milestone completion dates over time.

4. Earned Value charts: Graphical representation of planned value, earned value, and actual cost over time.

6.9. Risk Monitoring and Control

Risk monitoring and control involves implementing risk response plans, tracking identified risks, monitoring residual risks, identifying new risks, and evaluating the effectiveness of risk management processes throughout the project.

Reassessing Risks:

1. Regular risk reviews: Schedule periodic meetings to review and update the risk register.

2. New risk identification: Continuously scan for emerging risks throughout the project lifecycle.

3. Risk prioritization: Reassess risk priorities based on current project conditions and performance.

Implementing Risk Responses:

1. Trigger monitoring: Watch for early warning signs that signal a risk is about to occur.

2. Response execution: Implement planned risk responses when risk triggers occur.

3. Fallback plans: Activate secondary plans if primary risk responses prove ineffective.

Contingency Plan Execution:

1. Reserve analysis: Monitor the usage of contingency reserves for both time and cost.

2. Plan activation: Implement contingency plans when predefined thresholds are exceeded.

3. Performance tracking: Monitor the effectiveness of contingency plans and adjust as necessary.

6.10. Contract Administration and Procurement Monitoring

Contract administration involves managing relationships with sellers and ensuring all parties meet their contractual obligations.

Managing Vendor Relationships:

1. Regular communication: Maintain open lines of communication with vendors.

2. Performance reviews: Conduct periodic evaluations of vendor performance against contract requirements.

3. Issue resolution: Address any conflicts or performance issues promptly and professionally.

Contract Performance Monitoring:

1. Deliverable verification: Ensure that vendor deliverables meet specified requirements.

2. Payment processing: Review and approve vendor invoices in accordance with contract terms.

3. Change management: Handle any changes to contract scope, terms, or conditions through formal change control processes.

4. Documentation: Maintain comprehensive records of all contract-related communications and decisions.

By effectively implementing these monitoring and control processes, project managers can ensure that their projects stay on track, issues are identified and addressed promptly, and project objectives are met.

This comprehensive content covers the key aspects of project monitoring and control, providing a detailed guide on how to track project progress, manage changes, and ensure the project remains aligned with its objectives throughout its lifecycle.

SEVEN

PROJECT CLOSURE

7.1 Introduction to Project Closure

Project closure is the final phase of the project lifecycle, marking the formal completion of all project activities. This critical stage ensures that all project work is finished, deliverables are accepted, and resources are released. Proper project closure not only wraps up the current project but also provides valuable insights for future endeavours.

Key aspects of project closure:
- Formal acceptance of deliverables
- Administrative and financial closure
- Team dissolution and resource reallocation
- Lessons learned documentation
- Archiving project documents

The importance of a well-executed project closure cannot be overstated. It provides closure for team members, satisfies stakeholders, and contributes to organizational knowledge. This chapter will delve into the various components of project closure and provide best practices for ensuring a smooth and successful conclusion to your project.

7.2 Verifying Project Scope Completion

Before initiating the closure process, it's crucial to verify that all project scope requirements have been met. This involves:

1. Deliverable Review:
   - Compare final deliverables against the initial project scope statement
   - Ensure all features and functionalities are complete and operational
   - Verify that quality standards have been met
2. Requirements Traceability Matrix:

- Review the requirements traceability matrix to confirm all requirements have been fulfilled

- Address any discrepancies or incomplete items

3. Stakeholder Sign-off:

- Obtain formal sign-off from key stakeholders on all deliverables

- Document any outstanding issues or concerns

4. Scope Verification Checklist:

- Create and use a scope verification checklist to ensure thoroughness

- Include all major deliverables and project objectives in the checklist

5. Handling Scope Changes:

- Review and document any approved scope changes that occurred during the project

- Ensure all changes have been properly implemented and verified

6. Final Testing and Quality Assurance:

- Conduct final tests or quality checks as necessary

- Address any last-minute issues or bugs

By meticulously verifying project scope completion, you set the stage for a smooth transition into the formal closure process.

7.3 Obtaining Formal Acceptance

Securing formal acceptance of the project deliverables is a crucial step in project closure. This process involves:

1. Preparation of Acceptance Documents:

- Create formal acceptance documents that outline all deliverables

- Include project objectives, success criteria, and how they were met

2. Stakeholder Review:

- Allow stakeholders sufficient time to review the final deliverables

- Be available to answer questions or provide clarifications

3. Acceptance Meeting:

- Schedule a formal acceptance meeting with key stakeholders

- Present the final deliverables and project outcomes

- Address any final concerns or questions

4. Signing of Acceptance Documents:

- Obtain signatures from authorized stakeholders on the acceptance documents

- Ensure all parties have copies of the signed documents

5. Handling Conditional Acceptance:

- If there are minor outstanding items, consider conditional acceptance

- Clearly document any conditions and set deadlines for their resolution

6. Escalation Process:

- Have a clear escalation process in place for handling any acceptance disputes

Formal acceptance provides a clear demarcation of project completion and protects both the project team and the organization from future disputes.

7.4 Administrative Closure

Administrative closure involves wrapping up all the project's administrative aspects. This includes:

1. Contract Closure:

- Review all contracts related to the project
- Ensure all contractual obligations have been met
- Formally close out contracts with vendors and suppliers
- Obtain formal releases or sign-offs from contractors

2. Financial Closure:

- Finalize all financial transactions
- Reconcile the project budget
- Ensure all invoices have been paid and all payments received
- Prepare final financial reports

3. Documentation Completion:

- Ensure all project documents are up-to-date and complete
- Compile and organize all project records
- Create a final project report summarizing the project's performance

4. Archiving Project Information:

- Determine what information needs to be retained and for how long
- Establish a system for easy retrieval of archived information
- Ensure compliance with organizational and regulatory requirements

5. Releasing Resources:

- Return any borrowed or rented equipment
- Release team members back to their functional managers or to other projects
- Close out any project-specific facilities or work spaces

6. Updating Organizational Process Assets:

- Update any organizational process assets based on project experiences
- This may include templates, guidelines, or best practices

7. Project Management Information System (PMIS) Update:

- Ensure all information in the PMIS is current and complete
- Close out the project in the PMIS

Thorough administrative closure ensures that all loose ends are tied up and the organization can move forward without lingering project-related issues.

7.5 Team Dissolution and Recognition

As the project comes to a close, it's important to properly dissolve the team and recognize their contributions:

1. Team Debriefing:
- Conduct a final team meeting to reflect on the project
- Discuss successes, challenges, and lessons learned
- Allow team members to share their experiences and insights

2. Performance Evaluations:
- Provide individual performance feedback to team members
- Document their contributions for future reference

3. Recognition and Rewards:
- Acknowledge individual and team achievements
- Consider both formal and informal recognition methods
- This could include certificates, awards, or a celebration event

4. Career Development Discussions:
- Discuss future career opportunities with team members
- Provide recommendations or referrals as appropriate

5. Reintegration Planning:
- Help team members transition back to their functional roles or new projects
- Coordinate with functional managers to ensure smooth transitions

6. Addressing Team Concerns:
- Be open to addressing any lingering concerns or issues team members may have
- Ensure team members feel valued and heard throughout the dissolution process

Proper team dissolution and recognition not only provides closure for the current project but also sets the stage for future project success by maintaining team morale and engagement.

7.6 Lessons Learned Documentation

Documenting lessons learned is a critical part of project closure that contributes to organizational knowledge and improves future project performance. The process includes:

1. Lessons Learned Session:

- Schedule a dedicated lessons learned session with the project team and key stakeholders
- Create an open and non-judgmental environment for honest discussion

2. Areas to Cover:
- Project management processes
- Technical aspects of the project
- Team dynamics and communication
- Stakeholder management
- Risk management effectiveness
- Resource allocation and utilization
- Schedule and budget performance

3. Structured Approach:
- Use a structured format to capture lessons learned, such as:
- What worked well?
- What didn't work well?
- What would we do differently next time?
- What surprised us?

4. Documentation Methods:
- Use templates or forms to standardize the capture of lessons learned
- Consider using mind mapping or affinity diagramming techniques during the session

5. Quantitative and Qualitative Data:
- Include both quantitative data (e.g., schedule and budget variances) and qualitative insights

6. Action Items:
- Identify specific actions that can be taken to implement lessons learned in future projects

7. Dissemination:
- Determine how lessons learned will be shared within the organization
- Consider creating a lessons learned database or knowledge repository

8. Follow-up:
- Establish a process for reviewing and implementing lessons learned in future projects

By thoroughly documenting lessons learned, organizations can continuously improve their project management practices and increase the likelihood of future project success.

7.7 Post-Project Review

The post-project review, sometimes called a post-implementation review, evaluates the project's overall success and impact. This review typically occurs a few months after project closure and includes:

1. Objectives of the Post-Project Review:
- Assess if the project achieved its intended business benefits
- Evaluate the project's impact on the organization
- Identify any unforeseen consequences or benefits

2. Key Areas to Evaluate:
- Achievement of project objectives
- Realization of expected benefits
- User/customer satisfaction
- Operational performance of deliverables
- Return on investment (ROI)

3. Conducting the Review:
- Gather data from various sources (e.g., user surveys, operational reports)
- Interview key stakeholders and end-users
- Analyse project documentation and metrics

4. Review Team:
- Consider using an independent review team for objectivity
- Include representatives from different areas impacted by the project

5. Reporting:
- Prepare a comprehensive post-project review report
- Include findings, recommendations, and lessons learned

6. Action Planning:
- Develop action plans based on the review findings
- Assign responsibilities for implementing improvements

7. Knowledge Sharing:
- Share the results of the post-project review with relevant parties in the organization
- Use findings to inform future project planning and execution

The post-project review provides valuable insights into the long-term impact and success of the project, helping organizations maximize the benefits of their project investments.

7.8 Celebrating Project Completion

Celebrating the completion of a project is often overlooked but is an important part of project closure. It provides a sense of accomplishment, boosts morale, and helps transition the team to new endeavours.

1. Importance of Celebration:
- Recognizes team efforts and achievements
- Provides closure for team members
- Reinforces positive organizational culture

2. Types of Celebrations:
- Formal events (e.g., award ceremonies, dinners)
- Informal gatherings (e.g., team lunches, recreational activities)
- Virtual celebrations for remote teams

3. Involving Stakeholders:
- Consider including key stakeholders in the celebration
- Use the opportunity to strengthen relationships

4. Recognition and Awards:
- Acknowledge outstanding contributions
- Consider both team and individual recognitions

5. Sharing Success Stories:
- Use the celebration as an opportunity to share project success stories
- Highlight key achievements and their impact on the organization

Remember, the style and scale of the celebration should be appropriate to the project's size, duration, and significance to the organization.

7.9 Conclusion: Ensuring Long-term Project Success

Effective project closure is more than just a final checklist; it's a crucial process that sets the stage for future success. By properly closing a project, you:

1. Ensure Complete Delivery:
- Verify that all project objectives have been met
- Confirm stakeholder satisfaction with deliverables

2. Protect Against Future Disputes:
- Obtain formal acceptance and sign-offs
- Properly close contracts and financial accounts

3. Capture Valuable Knowledge:
- Document lessons learned for future reference
- Contribute to organizational process improvements

4. Recognize and Motivate Team Members:
- Acknowledge individual and team contributions
- Build a positive culture for future projects

5. Evaluate Long-term Impact:
- Assess the project's actual benefits through post-project reviews
- Identify areas for ongoing improvement

6. Facilitate Organizational Learning:
- Share project experiences and best practices
- Contribute to the organization's project management maturity
7. Provide Closure:
- Give team members and stakeholders a sense of completion
- Allow for smooth transitions to new projects or roles

Remember, the effort invested in proper project closure pays dividends in future project success and organizational growth. By following the steps outlined in this chapter, project managers can ensure that their projects end as successfully as they began, leaving a positive legacy and setting the stage for future achievements.

EIGHT

PROJECT SCOPE MANAGEMENT

8.1 Introduction to Project Scope Management

Project scope management is the process of defining and controlling what is and is not included in a project. It ensures that the project includes all the work required, and only the work required, to complete the project successfully.

Key components of scope management:
- Scope planning
- Scope definition
- Creating the Work Breakdown Structure (WBS)
- Scope verification
- Scope control

8.2 Defining Project Scope
8.2.1 Scope Statement
The scope statement is a crucial document that provides a detailed description of the project deliverables and the work required to create those deliverables. It typically includes:
- Project objectives
- Product scope description
- Project requirements
- Project boundaries
- Project deliverables

- Project exclusions
- Constraints and assumptions

8.2.2 Techniques for Defining Scope

- Stakeholder interviews
- Focus groups
- Workshops
- Questionnaires and surveys
- Prototypes or models
- Benchmarking against similar projects

8.2.3 Product Analysis

Breaking down the project's end product into smaller, more manageable components to better understand its characteristics and requirements.

8.3 Creating a Work Breakdown Structure (WBS)

8.3.1 Definition of WBS

A Work Breakdown Structure is a hierarchical decomposition of the total scope of work to be carried out by the project team to accomplish the project objectives and create the required deliverables.

8.3.2 Purpose of WBS

- Organizes and defines the total scope of the project
- Breaks work into manageable chunks
- Provides a framework for detailed cost, schedule, and resource planning
- Facilitates assignment of responsibilities
- Allows for more accurate estimation of time, cost, and resources

8.3.3 Creating a WBS

Steps to create a WBS:

1. Identify the final deliverables
2. Break down high-level deliverables into smaller components
3. Continue breaking down until you reach manageable work packages
4. Review and refine the WBS

8.3.4 WBS Dictionary

A document that provides detailed information about each component in the WBS, including:

- Description of work
- Responsible organization
- Schedule milestones

- Associated activities
- Resources required
- Cost estimates
- Quality requirements
- Acceptance criteria

8.4 Scope Control and Change Management

8.4.1 Scope Creep
Scope creep refers to uncontrolled changes or continuous growth in a project's scope. It can lead to:
- Project delays
- Budget overruns
- Resource conflicts
- Decreased stakeholder satisfaction

8.4.2 Change Control Process
Steps in the change control process:
1. Identify the proposed change
2. Review and evaluate the change request
3. Approve or reject the change
4. Update project documents if the change is approved
5. Communicate the change decision to stakeholders
6. Implement the approved change

8.4.3 Tools for Scope Control
- Variance analysis
- Trend analysis
- Performance measurement
- Project management software

8.5 Scope Verification

8.5.1 Definition
Scope verification is the process of formally accepting the completed project deliverables.

8.5.2 Techniques for Scope Verification
- Inspection
- Testing
- Demonstrations

- Peer reviews
- User acceptance testing

8.5.3 Importance of Scope Verification
- Ensures project deliverables meet requirements
- Reduces the risk of scope creep
- Increases stakeholder satisfaction
- Facilitates formal project closure

Conclusion:

Effective project scope management is crucial for project success. It ensures that all necessary work is included in the project while preventing unnecessary work from creeping in. By clearly defining the project scope, creating a detailed WBS, and implementing robust change control processes, project managers can keep their projects on track and increase the likelihood of meeting project objectives within the defined constraints of time, cost, and quality. In the next chapter, we will explore Time Management in Projects, another critical aspect of successful project management.

NINE

TIME MANAGEMENT IN PROJECTS

9.1 Introduction to Time Management

Time management in project management involves the processes required to manage the timely completion of the project. It includes:
- Defining activities
- Sequencing activities
- Estimating activity resources
- Estimating activity durations
- Developing the schedule
- Controlling the schedule

9.2 Activity Definition and Sequencing

9.2.1 Activity Definition

Activity definition involves identifying and documenting the specific actions to be performed to produce the project deliverables.
Techniques for activity definition:
- Decomposition
- Rolling wave planning
- Templates
- Expert judgment
Output: Activity list, a comprehensive list of all scheduled activities required on the project.

9.2.2 Activity Sequencing

Activity sequencing involves identifying and documenting relationships among project activities.

Types of dependencies:
- Finish-to-Start (FS): Activity B cannot start until Activity A is finished
- Start-to-Start (SS): Activity B cannot start until Activity A starts
- Finish-to-Finish (FF): Activity B cannot finish until Activity A is finished
- Start-to-Finish (SF): Activity B cannot finish until Activity A starts

Techniques for sequencing:
- Precedence Diagramming Method (PDM)
- Dependency Determination
- Applying leads and lags
Output: Project schedule network diagram

9.3 Schedule Development

9.3.1 Estimating Activity Resources

This process involves estimating the type and quantities of material, human resources, equipment, or supplies required to perform each activity.

Techniques:
- Expert judgment
- Alternative analysis
- Published estimating data
- Project management software

9.3.2 Estimating Activity Durations

This process involves estimating the number of work periods needed to complete individual activities with estimated resources.

Techniques:
- Expert judgment
- Analogous estimating
- Parametric estimating
- Three-point estimating (PERT)

9.3.3 Schedule Development

Schedule development involves analyzing activity sequences, durations, resource requirements, and schedule constraints to create the project schedule.

Techniques:
- Critical Path Method (CPM)
- Schedule compression
- What-if scenario analysis
- Resource leveling
- Critical chain method
Output: Project schedule

9.4 Critical Path Method (CPM)

9.4.1 Definition
The Critical Path Method is a technique used to determine the longest path of planned activities to the end of the project, and the earliest and latest that each activity can start and finish without making the project longer.

9.4.2 Steps in CPM:
1. List all activities
2. Determine dependencies
3. Draw the network diagram
4. Estimate duration for each activity
5. Identify the critical path
6. Calculate float (slack) for each activity

9.4.3 Importance of CPM
- Identifies which activities are "critical" (zero float)
- Helps in prioritizing resources
- Provides a visual representation of the project timeline
- Allows for schedule optimization

9.5 Time Estimation Techniques

9.5.1 Analogous Estimating

Using the actual duration of a similar previous project as the basis for estimating the duration of the current project.

9.5.2 Parametric Estimating

Using an algorithm to calculate cost or duration based on historical data and project parameters.

9.5.3 Three-Point Estimating (PERT)

Using three estimates to define an approximate range for an activity's duration:
- Most likely (M)
- Optimistic (O)
- Pessimistic (P)

PERT formula: $(O + 4M + P) / 6$

9.6 Schedule Control

9.6.1 Monitoring Project Progress

Techniques:
- Performance reviews
- Variance analysis
- Project management software

9.6.2 Managing Schedule Changes

Steps:
1. Identify the need for a change
2. Assess the impact of the change
3. Submit a change request
4. Review and approve/reject the change
5. Update the project schedule and related documents
6. Communicate the change to stakeholders

9.6.3 Schedule Compression Techniques

- Fast tracking: Performing activities in parallel that would normally be done in sequence

- Crashing: Adding resources to critical path activities to complete them in less time

9.7 Common Time Management Challenges
- Overoptimistic time estimates
- Failure to account for dependencies
- Inadequate risk management
- Poor resource allocation
- Scope creep
- Lack of buffer in the schedule

Conclusion:

Effective time management is crucial for project success. By accurately defining activities, estimating durations, developing a realistic schedule, and implementing robust control measures, project managers can ensure that their projects are completed on time. The techniques and methods discussed in this chapter provide a solid foundation for managing time effectively in projects. In the next chapter, we will explore Project Cost Management, another critical aspect of project management.

TEN

PROJECT COST MANAGEMENT

10.1 Introduction to Project Cost Management

Project Cost Management includes the processes involved in planning, estimating, budgeting, financing, funding, managing, and controlling costs so that the project can be completed within the approved budget. The main processes are:
- Cost estimation
- Cost budgeting
- Cost control

10.2 Cost Estimation

10.2.1 Definition

Cost estimation is the process of developing an approximation of the monetary resources needed to complete project activities.

10.2.2 Types of Cost Estimates
- Rough Order of Magnitude (ROM): -25% to +75%
- Budget Estimate: -10% to +25%
- Definitive Estimate: -5% to +10%

10.2.3 Cost Estimation Techniques
1. Analogous Estimating
- Using the actual cost of a similar previous project
- Quick but less accurate

- Useful when there's limited project information
2. Parametric Estimating
- Using statistical relationships between historical data and variables
- More accurate than analogous estimating
- Example: Cost per square foot in construction
3. Bottom-up Estimating
- Estimating individual work packages and rolling up
- Most accurate but time-consuming
- Requires detailed project information
4. Three-Point Estimating
- Uses optimistic, most likely, and pessimistic estimates
- Formula: (Optimistic + 4 x Most Likely + Pessimistic) / 6
5. Expert Judgment
- Relying on experts with relevant experience
- Useful when other techniques are not applicable

10.2.4 Factors Affecting Cost Estimates
- Project scope
- Resource availability and rates
- Time constraints
- Risk factors
- Market conditions
- Currency exchange rates (for international projects)

10.3 Cost Budgeting

10.3.1 Definition
Cost budgeting is the process of aggregating the estimated costs of individual activities or work packages to establish an authorized cost baseline.

10.3.2 Components of a Project Budget
- Direct costs: Costs directly attributable to the project (e.g., labor, materials)
- Indirect costs: Overhead costs (e.g., utilities, management salaries)
- Contingency reserve: Funds for identified risks
- Management reserve: Funds for unidentified risks

10.3.3 Creating a Cost Baseline

1. Sum up estimated costs for each work package
2. Add contingency reserves
3. Determine cost baseline curve (S-curve)

10.4 Cost Control

10.4.1 Definition

Cost control involves monitoring the status of the project to update the project budget and manage changes to the cost baseline.

10.4.2 Earned Value Management (EVM)

EVM is a technique that measures project performance and progress in an objective manner. Key components:
- Planned Value (PV): Budgeted cost of scheduled work
- Earned Value (EV): Budgeted cost of work performed
- Actual Cost (AC): Actual cost of work performed
EVM Calculations:
- Cost Variance (CV) = EV - AC
- Schedule Variance (SV) = EV - PV
- Cost Performance Index (CPI) = EV / AC
- Schedule Performance Index (SPI) = EV / PV
Interpreting EVM:
- CV > 0 and CPI > 1: Under budget
- CV < 0 and CPI < 1: Over budget
- SV > 0 and SPI > 1: Ahead of schedule
- SV < 0 and SPI < 1: Behind schedule

10.4.3 Forecasting
- Estimate at Completion (EAC): Projected total cost at project completion
- EAC = BAC / CPI (where BAC is Budget at Completion)

10.4.4 Change Control Process
1. Identify the need for a cost change
2. Evaluate the impact of the change
3. Submit a change request
4. Review and approve/reject the change
5. Update the project budget and related documents
6. Communicate the change to stakeholders

10.5 Cost Management Challenges

10.5.1 Common Challenges
- Inaccurate initial estimates
- Scope creep leading to cost overruns
- Unexpected risks materializing
- Poor cost tracking and control
- Currency fluctuations in international projects

10.5.2 Strategies to Overcome Challenges
- Use multiple estimation techniques
- Implement robust change control processes
- Regularly update and review cost estimates
- Maintain clear communication with stakeholders
- Use project management software for cost tracking

10.6 Cost Management Best Practices
- Involve team members in the estimation process
- Document all assumptions and constraints
- Regularly update cost forecasts
- Use historical data to improve future estimates
- Conduct post-project reviews to capture lessons learned

Conclusion:

Effective cost management is crucial for project success. By accurately estimating costs, creating a realistic budget, and implementing robust control measures, project managers can ensure that their projects are completed within the approved budget. The techniques and methods discussed in this chapter provide a solid foundation for managing costs effectively in projects. In the next chapter, we will explore Quality Management in Projects, another critical aspect of project management.

ELEVEN

QUALITY MANAGEMENT IN PROJECTS

11.1 Introduction to Quality Management

Quality management in projects involves the processes for incorporating the organization's quality policy regarding planning, managing, and controlling project and product quality requirements to meet stakeholders' objectives. It consists of three main processes:
- Quality Planning
- Quality Assurance
- Quality Control

11.2 Quality Planning

11.2.1 Definition
Quality planning is the process of identifying quality requirements and standards for the project and its deliverables, and documenting how the project will demonstrate compliance with quality requirements.

11.2.2 Key Components of Quality Planning
- Identifying relevant quality standards
- Determining quality objectives
- Defining quality metrics

- Creating a quality management plan

11.2.3 Tools and Techniques for Quality Planning
1. Cost-Benefit Analysis: Comparing the cost of quality activities to the expected benefits
2. Benchmarking: Comparing project practices to those of other projects
3. Design of Experiments: Statistical method for identifying factors that influence specific variables
4. Cost of Quality (COQ): Costs incurred to prevent, appraise, and correct defective work

11.2.4 Quality Management Plan
The quality management plan describes how the project management team will implement the organization's quality policy. It typically includes:
- Quality standards to be used
- Quality objectives
- Quality roles and responsibilities
- Quality tools and techniques to be used
- Major procedures relevant to quality

11.3 Quality Assurance

11.3.1 Definition
Quality assurance is the process of auditing the quality requirements and the results from quality control measurements to ensure that appropriate quality standards and operational definitions are used.

11.3.2 Key Components of Quality Assurance
- Process analysis
- Quality audits
- Continuous improvement

11.3.3 Tools and Techniques for Quality Assurance
1. Affinity Diagrams: Grouping large numbers of ideas into categories
2. Process Decision Program Charts (PDPC): Mapping out every conceivable event and contingency
3. Interrelationship Digraphs: Identifying logical relationships among related factors

4. Tree Diagrams: Breaking down broad categories into finer levels of detail

11.3.4 Quality Audits

Quality audits are structured, independent reviews to determine whether project activities comply with organizational and project policies, processes, and procedures. Objectives include:
- Identifying good practices
- Identifying gaps and shortcomings
- Sharing good practices
- Proactively offering assistance to improve processes
- Highlighting contributions of each audit in the lessons learned repository

11.4 Quality Control

11.4.1 Definition

Quality control is the process of monitoring and recording results of executing the quality activities to assess performance and recommend necessary changes.

11.4.2 Key Components of Quality Control
- Measuring project results
- Comparing results to quality standards
- Identifying causes of unsatisfactory results
- Recommending corrective actions

11.4.3 Tools and Techniques for Quality Control
1. Cause and Effect Diagrams (Ishikawa or Fishbone Diagrams): Identifying potential causes of defects
2. Control Charts: Determining whether a process is stable or predictable
3. Histograms: Showing the frequency distribution of variables
4. Scatter Diagrams: Showing the relationship between two variables
5. Pareto Charts: Identifying the vital few sources responsible for most problems
6. Statistical Sampling: Choosing part of a population for inspection
7. Inspection: Examining work products to determine if they conform to standards

11.5 Total Quality Management (TQM)

11.5.1 Definition

TQM is a management approach to long-term success through customer satisfaction. It is based on the participation of all members of an organization in improving processes, products, services, and the culture they work in.

11.5.2 Key Principles of TQM

- Customer focus
- Total employee involvement
- Process-centered
- Integrated system
- Strategic and systematic approach
- Continual improvement
- Fact-based decision making
- Communications

11.6 Six Sigma

11.6.1 Definition

Six Sigma is a data-driven approach for eliminating defects in any process. It aims to reduce variation in processes to achieve very high quality levels.

11.6.2 DMAIC Methodology

- Define: Define the problem, project goals, and customer requirements
- Measure: Measure the current process and collect relevant data
- Analyze: Analyze data to find root causes of defects and opportunities for improvement
- Improve: Implement and verify the solution
- Control: Control the future process to ensure defects don't recur

11.7 Challenges in Quality Management

11.7.1 Common Challenges

- Balancing quality with time and cost constraints
- Resistance to change in implementing quality processes
- Lack of management support
- Inadequate training or resources

- Difficulty in measuring quality in some project types

11.7.2 Strategies to Overcome Challenges
- Emphasize the long-term benefits of quality management
- Provide adequate training and resources
- Foster a culture of quality throughout the organization
- Use appropriate tools and techniques for the specific project
- Regularly review and improve quality processes

Conclusion:
Effective quality management is essential for project success and customer satisfaction. By implementing robust quality planning, assurance, and control processes, project managers can ensure that their projects meet or exceed stakeholder expectations. The techniques and methods discussed in this chapter provide a comprehensive approach to managing quality in projects. In the next chapter, we will explore Human Resource Management, another critical aspect of project management.

TWELVE
HUMAN RESOURCE MANAGEMENT

12.1 Introduction to Human Resource Management

Human Resource Management in project management involves the processes that organize, manage, and lead the project team. It includes:
- Planning human resource management
- Acquiring project team
- Developing project team
- Managing project team

12.2 Team Formation and Development

12.2.1 Stages of Team Development (Tuckman's Model)
1. Forming: Team members meet and learn about the project and their roles
2. Storming: Team members begin to address the project work, technical decisions, and approach
3. Norming: Team members begin to work together and adjust their work habits and behaviors
4. Performing: Teams are functioning well and members are interdependent
5. Adjourning: Team completes the work and moves on from the project

12.2.2 Team Building Activities
- Clear communication of goals
- Team-building exercises
- Establishing ground rules

- Clarifying roles and responsibilities
- Co-location or virtual team rooms
- Recognition and rewards

12.3 Roles and Responsibilities

12.3.1 Project Manager's Role
- Planning and defining project scope
- Building and leading project team
- Managing risks, issues, and changes
- Monitoring progress and performance
- Stakeholder communication
- Ensuring project deliverables meet quality standards

12.3.2 Team Member Roles
- Executing assigned tasks
- Collaborating with other team members
- Reporting progress and issues
- Contributing to problem-solving and decision-making
- Adhering to project processes and standards

12.3.3 Tools for Defining Roles and Responsibilities
- Responsibility Assignment Matrix (RAM)
- RACI Chart (Responsible, Accountable, Consulted, Informed)
- Text-oriented formats
- Organizational charts

12.4 Leadership in Project Management

12.4.1 Leadership Styles
- Autocratic: Leader makes all decisions
- Democratic: Team members participate in decision-making
- Laissez-faire: Team members have high autonomy
- Transformational: Leader inspires and motivates team
- Servant: Leader focuses on supporting and empowering team members

12.4.2 Key Leadership Skills for Project Managers
- Communication

- Motivation
- Decision-making
- Conflict resolution
- Emotional intelligence
- Adaptability

12.4.3 Motivating Project Teams
- Setting clear goals and expectations
- Providing regular feedback
- Recognizing and rewarding good performance
- Offering opportunities for growth and development
- Creating a positive work environment

12.5 Resource Management

12.5.1 Resource Planning
- Identifying required skills and expertise
- Estimating resource requirements
- Creating resource breakdown structure
- Developing resource calendars

12.5.2 Resource Acquisition
- Internal recruitment
- External hiring
- Contracting
- Virtual team considerations

12.5.3 Resource Allocation
- Assigning resources to project tasks
- Balancing workload across team members
- Managing resource conflicts
- Resource leveling and smoothing techniques

12.6 Performance Management

12.6.1 Setting Performance Expectations
- Defining clear objectives
- Establishing performance metrics

- Aligning individual goals with project goals

12.6.2 Performance Evaluation
- Regular check-ins and feedback
- Formal performance reviews
- 360-degree feedback

12.6.3 Managing Underperformance
- Identifying root causes
- Providing additional support or training
- Implementing performance improvement plans
- Taking corrective action when necessary

12.7 Conflict Management

12.7.1 Common Sources of Conflict
- Scarce resources
- Scheduling priorities
- Personal work styles
- Technical opinions
- Administrative procedures
- Cost

12.7.2 Conflict Resolution Techniques
- Confronting/Problem Solving: Directly addressing the conflict
- Compromising: Finding a solution that partially satisfies all parties
- Smoothing: Emphasizing areas of agreement
- Forcing: Using authority to resolve the conflict
- Withdrawing: Retreating from the conflict situation

12.8 Virtual Team Management

12.8.1 Challenges of Virtual Teams
- Communication barriers
- Time zone differences
- Cultural diversity
- Technology issues
- Building trust and relationships

12.8.2 Strategies for Managing Virtual Teams
- Utilizing appropriate communication tools
- Establishing clear communication protocols
- Regular virtual meetings
- Building team culture and cohesion
- Providing necessary technology and support

12.9 Human Resource Management Challenges

12.9.1 Common Challenges
- Limited resources
- Team member turnover
- Skill gaps
- Conflicts between team members
- Balancing project work with operational work

12.9.2 Strategies to Overcome Challenges
- Effective resource planning and allocation
- Continuous skill development and cross-training
- Implementing robust conflict resolution processes
- Maintaining open communication channels
- Regular team building activities

Conclusion:
Effective human resource management is crucial for project success. By implementing robust processes for team formation, development, and management, project managers can ensure that their teams are motivated, productive, and working towards project goals. The techniques and methods discussed in this chapter provide a comprehensive approach to managing human resources in projects. In the next chapter, we will explore Communication in Project Management, another critical aspect of successful project execution.

THIRTEEN
Communication in Project Management

13.1 Introduction to Project Communication

Communication is a critical factor in project success. It involves the processes required to ensure timely and appropriate planning, collection, creation, distribution, storage, retrieval, management, control, monitoring, and ultimate disposition of project information. Effective communication ensures that the right information reaches the right stakeholders at the right time.

13.2 Communication Planning

13.2.1 Developing a Communication Management Plan

The Communication Management Plan outlines:
- Stakeholder communication requirements
- Information to be communicated
- Reason for distribution of information
- Timeframe and frequency
- Person responsible for communication
- Person or groups who will receive the information
- Methods or technologies used to convey information
- Resources allocated for communication activities

- Escalation process for resolving issues

13.2.2 Communication Methods
- Interactive communication: Meetings, phone calls, video conferencing
- Push communication: Emails, letters, reports, memos
- Pull communication: Intranet sites, e-learning, knowledge repositories

13.2.3 Communication Channels
Number of communication channels = n(n-1)/2, where n is the number of stakeholders

13.3 Information Distribution

8.3.1 Types of Project Information
- Project status updates
- Technical documentation
- Project schedules
- Risk registers
- Change requests
- Meeting minutes
- Financial reports

13.3.2 Information Distribution Tools
- Project management information systems
- Collaborative work management tools
- Video conferencing
- Email and instant messaging
- Project websites
- Document management systems

13.4 Performance Reporting

13.4.1 Types of Performance Reports
- Status reports: Current state of the project
- Progress reports: Work accomplished in a given period
- Forecast reports: Future project status and progress
- Trend reports: Project performance over time
- Variance reports: Differences between planned and actual performance

13.4.2 Key Performance Indicators (KPIs)
- Schedule performance index (SPI)
- Cost performance index (CPI)
- Earned value metrics
- Quality metrics
- Risk response effectiveness

13.4.3 Reporting Techniques
- Data gathering and retrieval
- Data analysis
- Status meetings
- Dashboards and scorecards
- Variance analysis

13.5 Stakeholder Communication

13.5.1 Identifying Stakeholders
- Internal stakeholders: Team members, sponsors, executives
- External stakeholders: Clients, suppliers, government agencies

13.5.2 Stakeholder Analysis
- Power/Interest Grid
- Salience Model (Power, Urgency, Legitimacy)
- Stakeholder Engagement Assessment Matrix

13.5.3 Tailoring Communication
- Consider stakeholder preferences
- Adjust communication style and content based on stakeholder needs
- Use appropriate level of detail for each stakeholder group

13.6 Communication Skills for Project Managers

13.6.1 Active Listening
- Pay full attention to the speaker
- Provide feedback
- Defer judgment
- Respond appropriately

13.6.2 Non-verbal Communication
- Body language
- Eye contact
- Facial expressions
- Gestures

13.6.3 Presentation Skills
- Preparation and planning
- Effective use of visual aids
- Engaging delivery
- Handling questions and feedback

13.6.4 Writing Skills
- Clear and concise writing
- Appropriate tone and style
- Proper formatting and structure
- Proofreading and editing

13.7 Communication in Virtual Teams

13.7.1 Challenges
- Lack of face-to-face interaction
- Time zone differences
- Cultural and language barriers
- Technology limitations

13.7.2 Best Practices
- Establish clear communication protocols
- Use appropriate collaboration tools
- Schedule regular virtual meetings
- Encourage informal communication
- Be aware of cultural differences

13.8 Communication Barriers and How to Overcome Them

13.8.1 Common Barriers
- Language and cultural differences

- Information overload
- Lack of clear objectives
- Poor listening skills
- Assumptions and misinterpretations

13.8.2 Strategies to Overcome Barriers

- Use simple and clear language
- Encourage feedback and questions
- Verify understanding
- Be aware of cultural differences
- Use multiple communication channels

13.9 Communication Technology

13.9.1 Project Management Software

- Features for communication and collaboration
- Document sharing and version control
- Task assignment and tracking

13.9.2 Collaboration Platforms

- Team messaging apps
- Virtual whiteboards
- Shared calendars and task lists

13.9.3 Video Conferencing Tools

- Features for large team meetings
- Screen sharing capabilities
- Recording options for future reference

13.10 Measuring Communication Effectiveness

13.10.1 Metrics

- Stakeholder satisfaction surveys
- Communication audit results
- Project performance improvements
- Reduction in conflicts and misunderstandings

13.10.2 Continuous Improvement

- Regular review of communication processes
- Soliciting feedback from team members and stakeholders
- Adapting communication strategies based on project needs

Conclusion:

Effective communication is the cornerstone of successful project management. By implementing a comprehensive communication plan, utilizing appropriate tools and techniques, and continuously improving communication processes, project managers can ensure that all stakeholders are informed, engaged, and aligned with project objectives. The strategies and methods discussed in this chapter provide a robust framework for managing communication in projects of all sizes and complexities. In the next chapter, we will explore Risk Management, another critical aspect of project management.

FOURTEEN
RISK MANAGEMENT

14.1 Introduction to Risk Management

Risk management is the process of identifying, analyzing, and responding to project risks. It aims to increase the probability and impact of positive events and decrease the probability and impact of negative events in the project.

14.2 Risk Identification

14.2.1 Definition
Risk identification is the process of determining which risks may affect the project and documenting their characteristics.

14.2.2 Risk Identification Techniques
1. Brainstorming
2. Delphi technique
3. Interviewing
4. Root cause analysis
5. SWOT analysis (Strengths, Weaknesses, Opportunities, Threats)
6. Checklist analysis
7. Assumption analysis
8. Diagramming techniques (e.g., cause-and-effect diagrams, system or process flow charts)

14.2.3 Sources of Risk
- Technical risks

- Management risks
- Commercial risks
- External risks (e.g., regulatory, environmental)

14.2.4 Risk Register

The primary output of risk identification is the risk register, which includes:
- List of identified risks
- Potential risk owners
- List of potential risk responses

14.3 Risk Assessment

14.3.1 Qualitative Risk Analysis

Qualitative risk analysis prioritizes risks for further analysis by assessing their probability of occurrence and impact.
Techniques:
- Risk probability and impact assessment
- Risk categorization
- Risk urgency assessment
- Expert judgment
Tools:
- Probability and Impact Matrix
- Risk categorization

14.3.2 Quantitative Risk Analysis

Quantitative risk analysis numerically analyzes the effect of identified risks on overall project objectives.
Techniques:
- Sensitivity analysis
- Expected Monetary Value (EMV) analysis
- Decision tree analysis
- Monte Carlo simulation

14.4 Risk Response Planning

14.4.1 Risk Response Strategies for Negative Risks (Threats)

1. Avoid: Eliminate the threat by eliminating the cause
2. Transfer: Shift the impact of a threat to a third party

3. Mitigate: Reduce the probability or impact of a threat

4. Accept: Acknowledge the risk without taking any action

14.4.2 Risk Response Strategies for Positive Risks (Opportunities)

1. Exploit: Ensure the opportunity is realized

2. Enhance: Increase the probability or impact of an opportunity

3. Share: Allocate ownership to a third party who can best capture the opportunity

4. Accept: Take advantage of the opportunity if it arises, but don't pursue it

14.4.3 Contingency Planning

Developing a contingency plan or fallback plan for identified risks that occur despite attempts to avoid or reduce them.

14.4.4 Risk Response Plan

For each risk that will be actively managed, develop a risk response plan that includes:

- Risk description
- Risk owner
- Agreed response strategy
- Specific actions to implement the strategy
- Budget and timing
- Contingency plans

14.5 Risk Monitoring and Control

14.5.1 Risk Monitoring Techniques

- Risk reassessment
- Risk audits
- Variance and trend analysis
- Technical performance measurement
- Reserve analysis

14.5.2 Risk Reporting

- Regular risk review meetings
- Risk dashboard or heat map
- Updated risk register

14.5.3 Trigger Conditions
Identifying and monitoring risk triggers that indicate a risk is about to occur.

14.6 Proactive vs. Reactive Risk Management
- Proactive: Identifying and managing risks before they become problems
- Reactive: Dealing with risks as they occur
Benefits of proactive risk management:
- Reduced surprises
- More efficient use of resources
- Increased likelihood of project success

14.7 Risk Management in Agile Projects
- Continuous risk identification and assessment throughout sprints
- Use of risk burndown charts
- Incorporation of risk management into sprint planning and retrospectives

14.8 Risk Management Challenges

14.8.1 Common Challenges
- Incomplete risk identification
- Inaccurate risk assessment
- Lack of follow-through on risk responses
- Inadequate resources for risk management
- Resistance to acknowledging risks

14.8.2 Strategies to Overcome Challenges
- Foster a risk-aware culture
- Allocate sufficient time and resources for risk management
- Regularly review and update the risk register
- Integrate risk management into all project processes
- Provide risk management training to team members

14.9 Risk Management Best Practices
1. Start risk management early in the project
2. Communicate risks openly and regularly
3. Make risk management a continuous process

4. Involve the entire project team in risk management
5. Use both qualitative and quantitative risk analysis
6. Prioritize risks and focus on the most critical ones
7. Develop specific and actionable risk responses
8. Learn from past projects and use historical data
9. Balance the cost of risk management with potential benefits
10. Regularly review and update risk management processes

Conclusion:

Effective risk management is crucial for project success. By systematically identifying, assessing, and responding to risks, project managers can minimize threats and maximize opportunities. The techniques and methods discussed in this chapter provide a comprehensive approach to managing risks in projects of all sizes and complexities. In the next chapter, we will explore Procurement Management, another important aspect of project management.

FIFTEEN

PROCUREMENT MANAGEMENT

15.1 Introduction to Procurement Management

Procurement management involves the processes necessary to purchase or acquire products, services, or results needed from outside the project team. It includes:
- Planning procurement management
- Conducting procurements
- Controlling procurements
- Closing procurements

15.2 Procurement Planning

15.2.1 Make-or-Buy Analysis

Determining whether to make a product in-house or purchase it from an external source.
Considerations:
- Cost comparison
- Available resources and expertise
- Time constraints
- Strategic importance

15.2.2 Contract Types

1. Fixed-price contracts
- Firm Fixed Price (FFP)
- Fixed Price Incentive Fee (FPIF)

- Fixed Price with Economic Price Adjustment (FP-EPA)
2. Cost-reimbursable contracts
- Cost Plus Fixed Fee (CPFF)
- Cost Plus Incentive Fee (CPIF)
- Cost Plus Award Fee (CPAF)
3. Time and Materials (T&M) contracts

15.2.3 Procurement Management Plan

The plan outlines:
- Types of contracts to be used
- Risk management issues
- Standardized procurement documents
- Coordination with other project aspects
- Constraints and assumptions
- Handling multiple suppliers
- Metrics to manage suppliers

15.3 Conducting Procurements

15.3.1 Supplier Evaluation Criteria

- Understanding of need
- Overall cost
- Technical capability
- Risk
- Management approach
- Past performance

15.3.2 Supplier Selection Techniques

- Weighted averaging
- Independent estimates
- Screening systems
- Contract negotiations
- Seller rating systems

15.3.3 Procurement Documents

- Request for Information (RFI)
- Invitation for Bid (IFB)
- Request for Proposal (RFP)

- Request for Quotation (RFQ)

15.3.4 Source Selection
- Evaluating proposals
- Negotiating with suppliers
- Awarding contracts

15.4 Controlling Procurements

15.4.1 Contract Administration
- Managing the relationship with the seller
- Monitoring contract performance
- Making changes and corrections as needed

15.4.2 Performance Reporting
- Regular status reports from suppliers
- Performance reviews
- Inspections and audits

15.4.3 Payment Systems
- Advance payments
- Progress payments
- Retention

15.4.4 Claims Administration
- Identifying and resolving claims
- Preventing claims through proactive management

15.5 Closing Procurements

15.5.1 Procurement Audits
- Review of the procurement process
- Identification of successes and failures

15.5.2 Negotiated Settlements
- Resolving all open issues
- Finalizing all administrative matters

15.5.3 Records Management System
- Indexing contract documentation
- Archiving procurement records

15.6 Legal and Ethical Considerations

15.6.1 Contract Law
- Basic principles of contract law
- Breach of contract and remedies

15.6.2 Intellectual Property Rights
- Patents, copyrights, and trademarks
- Protecting proprietary information

15.6.3 Ethical Considerations
- Conflict of interest
- Fair competition
- Confidentiality
- Anti-corruption practices

15.7 International Procurement

15.7.1 Cultural Considerations
- Understanding local business practices
- Communication challenges

15.7.2 Legal and Regulatory Issues
- Import/export regulations
- Local content requirements
- Currency exchange considerations

15.7.3 Global Supply Chain Management
- Managing international logistics
- Dealing with time zone differences

15.8 E-Procurement

15.8.1 Benefits of E-Procurement
- Increased efficiency
- Cost savings
- Improved transparency
- Better spend analysis

15.8.2 E-Procurement Tools
- Online marketplaces
- E-auctions
- Supplier portals
- Contract management software

15.9 Procurement Risks and Mitigation Strategies

15.9.1 Common Procurement Risks
- Supplier bankruptcy
- Quality issues
- Delivery delays
- Cost overruns
- Scope creep

15.9.2 Risk Mitigation Strategies
- Thorough due diligence
- Performance bonds
- Multiple sourcing
- Clear contract terms and conditions
- Regular supplier evaluations

15.10 Best Practices in Procurement Management
1. Develop a clear procurement strategy aligned with project goals
2. Conduct thorough market research
3. Establish clear evaluation criteria for supplier selection
4. Maintain open and regular communication with suppliers
5. Implement robust contract management processes
6. Continuously monitor and evaluate supplier performance
7. Foster long-term relationships with key suppliers
8. Stay updated on procurement regulations and best practices

9. Leverage technology to streamline procurement processes
10. Integrate procurement management with overall project management

Conclusion:
Effective procurement management is crucial for acquiring the necessary resources and services for project success. By implementing a structured approach to planning, conducting, controlling, and closing procurements, project managers can ensure that their projects receive high-quality deliverables while managing costs and risks. The techniques and best practices discussed in this chapter provide a comprehensive framework for managing procurements in projects of all sizes and complexities. In the next chapter, we will explore Project Management Tools and Techniques, which will provide an overview of various tools that can be used across all knowledge areas of project management.

SIXTEEN

PROJECT MANAGEMENT TOOLS AND TECHNIQUES

16.1 Introduction to Project Management Tools and Techniques
This chapter covers various tools and techniques used across different knowledge areas of project management. These tools help project managers plan, execute, monitor, and control projects effectively.

16.2 Gantt Charts

16.2.1 Definition
A Gantt chart is a horizontal bar chart that visually represents project tasks against time.

16.2.2 Components
- Tasks or activities
- Start and end dates
- Duration
- Dependencies
- Milestones

16.2.3 Benefits
- Visual representation of project schedule
- Easy to understand and communicate

- Shows task dependencies
- Helps in resource allocation

16.2.4 Creating a Gantt Chart
- List all tasks
- Determine task durations
- Identify dependencies
- Set milestones
- Input data into project management software

16.3 PERT Diagrams

16.3.1 Definition
Program Evaluation and Review Technique (PERT) is a method to analyze the tasks involved in completing a project.

16.3.2 Components
- Activities
- Dependencies
- Time estimates (optimistic, pessimistic, most likely)

16.3.3 PERT Formula
Expected time = (Optimistic + 4 × Most Likely + Pessimistic) ÷ 6

16.3.4 Benefits
- Provides a visual representation of task dependencies
- Helps identify the critical path
- Allows for probabilistic time estimates

16.4 Critical Path Method (CPM)

16.4.1 Definition
CPM is a technique used to predict project duration by analyzing which sequence of activities has the least amount of scheduling flexibility.

16.4.2 Steps in CPM
1. List all activities
2. Determine dependencies

3. Estimate duration for each activity
4. Calculate early start, early finish, late start, and late finish for each activity
5. Identify the critical path
6. Calculate float for each activity

16.4.3 Benefits
- Identifies critical activities that directly impact project duration
- Helps in schedule compression
- Allows for effective resource allocation

16.5 Work Breakdown Structure (WBS)

16.5.1 Definition
A WBS is a hierarchical decomposition of the total scope of work to be carried out by the project team.

16.5.2 Components
- Deliverables
- Work packages
- WBS Dictionary

16.5.3 Creating a WBS
1. Identify major deliverables
2. Decompose deliverables into smaller components
3. Assign unique identifiers to each element
4. Verify that decomposition is sufficient

16.5.4 Benefits
- Provides a framework for detailed cost estimating and control
- Defines scope of work
- Facilitates clear responsibility assignments

16.6 Project Management Software

16.6.1 Types of Software
- Desktop applications (e.g., Microsoft Project)
- Web-based tools (e.g., Asana, Trello)
- Enterprise project management solutions

16.6.2 Common Features
- Scheduling
- Resource management
- Cost tracking
- Reporting and analytics
- Collaboration tools

16.6.3 Selecting Project Management Software
- Assess project needs
- Consider team size and location
- Evaluate integration capabilities
- Review user-friendliness
- Consider cost and scalability

16.7 Earned Value Management (EVM)

16.7.1 Definition
EVM is a project management technique for measuring project performance and progress in an objective manner.

16.7.2 Key Components
- Planned Value (PV)
- Earned Value (EV)
- Actual Cost (AC)

16.7.3 EVM Calculations
- Schedule Variance (SV) = EV - PV
- Cost Variance (CV) = EV - AC
- Schedule Performance Index (SPI) = EV / PV
- Cost Performance Index (CPI) = EV / AC

16.7.4 Benefits
- Provides early warning signals
- Enables forecasting of project performance
- Integrates schedule and cost performance

16.8 Risk Management Tools

16.8.1 Risk Register
- List of identified risks
- Potential responses
- Risk owners

16.8.2 Risk Probability and Impact Matrix
- Qualitative risk analysis tool
- Combines probability and impact scores

16.8.3 Decision Trees
- Quantitative risk analysis tool
- Helps in decision-making under uncertainty

16.9 Communication Tools

16.9.1 Project Dashboard
- Visual representation of key project metrics
- Typically includes schedule, budget, and scope status

16.9.2 Stakeholder Analysis Matrix
- Identifies and analyzes stakeholder influence and interest
- Helps in developing communication strategies

16.9.3 Communication Plan
- Outlines what, when, how, and to whom information will be distributed

16.10 Quality Management Tools

16.10.1 Cause-and-Effect Diagrams (Ishikawa or Fishbone Diagrams)
- Identifies potential causes of problems

16.10.2 Control Charts
- Determines whether a process is stable and predictable

16.10.3 Pareto Charts
- Identifies the vital few sources responsible for most problems

16.11 Agile Project Management Tools

16.11.1 Kanban Boards
- Visual representation of work at various stages of a process

16.11.2 Burndown Charts
- Shows work completed against time

16.11.3 User Stories
- Simple descriptions of features from an end-user perspective

16.12 Resource Management Tools

16.12.1 Resource Histograms
- Displays resource usage over time

16.12.2 RACI Matrix (Responsible, Accountable, Consulted, Informed)
- Clarifies roles and responsibilities for each project task

16.13 Best Practices for Using Project Management Tools
1. Choose tools that fit your project and organizational needs
2. Ensure proper training for team members
3. Use tools consistently across projects
4. Regularly update and maintain project data
5. Integrate tools with existing systems when possible
6. Don't rely solely on tools – use them to support good project management practices
7. Regularly review and assess the effectiveness of tools
8. Be open to adopting new tools as project needs evolve

Conclusion:
Project management tools and techniques are essential for planning, executing, and controlling projects effectively. By leveraging these tools, project managers can improve communication, track progress, manage resources, and increase the likelihood of project success. The tools and techniques discussed in this chapter provide a comprehensive toolkit for managing projects of various sizes and complexities. Remember that while

these tools are valuable, they should be used in conjunction with sound project management principles and practices.

Agile Project Management

1. Intoduction

In the fast-paced and ever-evolving world of project management, Agile methodologies have emerged as a transformative approach to managing projects. Agile Project Management is not just a set of processes; it's a mindset, a way of thinking that prioritizes flexibility, collaboration, and customer satisfaction. This chapter provides an introduction to Agile Project Management, exploring its origins, core principles, methodologies, and benefits.

2. What is Agile Project Management?

Agile Project Management is an iterative and incremental approach to managing projects. It emphasizes flexibility, customer collaboration, and rapid delivery of functional product increments. Unlike traditional methodologies that follow a linear, sequential process, Agile is adaptive, allowing project teams to respond to changing requirements and feedback throughout the project lifecycle.

3. Origins and Core Values of Agile

The Agile methodology was formally introduced in 2001 with the creation of the Agile Manifesto by a group of software developers. The manifesto outlines four core values and twelve principles that form the foundation of Agile practices. The core values are:

Individuals and interactions over processes and tools: Emphasizing the importance of human elements in the project, Agile values team collaboration and communication above rigid processes and tools.

Working software over comprehensive documentation: Prioritizing functional deliverables that meet customer needs, Agile focuses on creating working products rather than exhaustive documentation.

Customer collaboration over contract negotiation: Agile encourages ongoing engagement with customers to ensure the project aligns with their evolving needs and expectations.

Responding to change over following a plan: Recognizing that change is inevitable, Agile methodologies are designed to be flexible and adaptive, allowing teams to adjust plans as new information and requirements emerge.

4. Key Principles of Agile Project Management

Agile principles extend these values into actionable guidelines that govern the behavior and practices of Agile teams. Some key principles include:

Customer satisfaction through early and continuous delivery: By delivering valuable, functional increments of the project early and regularly, Agile ensures that customers are consistently engaged and satisfied.

Welcome changing requirements, even late in development: Agile teams embrace change as an opportunity to enhance the product's value, adapting plans to accommodate new insights and needs.

Deliver working software frequently: Regular, incremental releases ensure that progress is tangible and that customers receive value sooner.

Close, daily cooperation between business stakeholders and developers: Agile emphasizes strong collaboration between the development team and business stakeholders to maintain alignment and address issues promptly.

Build projects around motivated individuals: Empowering team members, Agile creates an environment where individuals are trusted and supported, leading to higher motivation and better performance.

Face-to-face communication: Recognizing that direct communication is the most effective form of conveying information, Agile teams prioritize face-to-face interactions.

Working software is the primary measure of progress: Agile focuses on delivering functional products as the main indicator of project progress, rather than on secondary metrics like documentation or meetings.

Sustainable development: Agile promotes a pace of work that can be maintained indefinitely, avoiding burnout and ensuring long-term productivity.

Continuous attention to technical excellence: Agile teams strive for high-quality code and robust design, enhancing the product's overall quality and maintainability.

Simplicity—the art of maximizing the amount of work not done: By focusing on essential features and avoiding unnecessary work, Agile teams streamline their efforts and deliver more value.

Self-organizing teams: Agile teams are self-organizing, taking ownership of their work and fostering innovation and accountability.

Regular reflection and adjustment: Agile teams continuously reflect on their performance and processes, making adjustments to improve efficiency and effectiveness.

5. Agile Methodologies

Agile encompasses various methodologies, each with its own practices and tools but all aligned with the core Agile values and principles. Some of the most popular Agile methodologies include:

Scrum: Scrum is a framework that structures project work into sprints, typically lasting two to four weeks. Key roles in Scrum include the Product Owner, Scrum Master, and Development Team. Scrum emphasizes iterative progress, regular reviews, and daily stand-up meetings to ensure transparency and continuous improvement.

Kanban: Kanban focuses on visualizing the workflow and managing work in progress. Using a Kanban board, teams track tasks through various stages of completion, aiming to improve flow and identify bottlenecks.

Lean: Lean methodology seeks to maximize value by eliminating waste and optimizing processes. It emphasizes continuous improvement, efficient use of resources, and delivering value to the customer.

Extreme Programming (XP): XP is an Agile methodology that emphasizes technical excellence and frequent releases. It includes practices such as pair programming, test-driven development, and continuous integration to ensure high-quality code and responsiveness to change.

6. Benefits of Agile Project Management

Adopting Agile Project Management offers numerous benefits:

Enhanced Flexibility and Adaptability: Agile's iterative approach allows teams to adjust plans and priorities based on feedback and changing requirements, leading to better alignment with customer needs.

Improved Collaboration and Communication: Regular interactions between team members and stakeholders foster a collaborative environment, enhancing understanding and problem-solving.

Faster Time to Market: By delivering functional increments regularly, Agile teams can bring products to market more quickly, gaining a competitive advantage.

Increased Customer Satisfaction: Ongoing customer involvement and regular delivery of valuable products ensure that the final outcome meets or exceeds customer expectations.

Higher Quality Products: Continuous testing, feedback, and iteration improve product quality, reducing the likelihood of defects and rework.

Empowered Teams: Agile empowers team members to take ownership of their work, leading to higher motivation, accountability, and productivity.

7. Conclusion

Agile Project Management represents a paradigm shift in how projects are managed, prioritizing flexibility, collaboration, and continuous improvement. By adopting Agile principles and methodologies, organizations can navigate the complexities of modern project environments, deliver high-quality products, and achieve greater customer satisfaction. As you delve deeper into Agile practices in the subsequent chapters, you will gain the knowledge and skills needed to implement Agile successfully in your projects, driving efficiency, innovation, and value.

SEVENTEEN

INTRODUCTION TO AGILE PROJECT MANAGEMENT

17.1. The Origins of Agile

The roots of Agile project management can be traced back to the software development industry in the 1990s. During this time, many software projects were failing due to rigid, linear approaches that couldn't adapt to changing requirements and market conditions.

In February 2001, a group of 17 software developers met at the Snowbird ski resort in Utah to discuss lightweight development methods. This meeting led to the creation of the Agile Manifesto, a document that would revolutionize project management, particularly in software development.

Key figures in this meeting included Kent Beck, Ken Schwaber, and Jeff Sutherland, who would go on to develop specific Agile methodologies like Extreme Programming (XP) and Scrum.

17.2. The Agile Manifesto

The Agile Manifesto consists of four core values:

a) Individuals and interactions over processes and tools

This value emphasizes the importance of team dynamics and communication. While processes and tools are necessary, they should support and enhance human collaboration rather than hinder it.

b) Working software over comprehensive documentation

The focus should be on delivering functional software rather than extensive documentation. Documentation is still important, but it should not be prioritized over working products.

c) Customer collaboration over contract negotiation

This value stresses the importance of involving customers throughout the development process, rather than relying solely on initial contract specifications.

d) Responding to change over following a plan

Agile methodologies embrace change, recognizing that requirements often evolve during a project. This flexibility allows teams to adapt to new information and changing market conditions.

It's important to note that while the manifesto values the items on the right, it recognizes that the items on the left are more valuable in delivering successful projects.

17.3. The Twelve Principles of Agile

The Agile Manifesto is supported by twelve principles:

1. Our highest priority is to satisfy the customer through early and continuous delivery of valuable software.

2. Welcome changing requirements, even late in development. Agile processes harness change for the customer's competitive advantage.

3. Deliver working software frequently, from a couple of weeks to a couple of months, with a preference to the shorter timescale.

4. Business people and developers must work together daily throughout the project.

5. Build projects around motivated individuals. Give them the environment and support they need, and trust them to get the job done.

6. The most efficient and effective method of conveying information to and within a development team is face-to-face conversation.

7. Working software is the primary measure of progress.

8. Agile processes promote sustainable development. The sponsors, developers, and users should be able to maintain a constant pace indefinitely.

9. Continuous attention to technical excellence and good design enhances agility.

10. Simplicity--the art of maximizing the amount of work not done--is essential.

11. The best architectures, requirements, and designs emerge from self-organizing teams.

12. At regular intervals, the team reflects on how to become more effective, then tunes and adjusts its behavior accordingly.

These principles guide Agile practices, emphasizing customer satisfaction, adaptability, regular delivery of working products, collaboration, trust in team members, effective communication, sustainable pace, technical excellence, simplicity, self-organization, and continuous improvement.

17.4. Agile vs. Traditional Project Management

Agile project management differs significantly from traditional (often called "Waterfall") approaches:

Aspect	Traditional	Agile
Project phases	Sequential	Iterative
Requirements	Defined upfront	Evolve over time
Customer involvement	Mainly at start and end	Continuous
Deliverables	One final product	Incremental releases
Changes	Resisted	Welcomed
Planning	Extensive upfront	Continuous
Documentation	Comprehensive	Just enough
Success measure	Adherence to plan	Customer satisfaction

Traditional vs Agile Project Management

While traditional methods follow a linear path from requirements gathering to delivery, Agile approaches work in short iterations, continuously refining the product based on feedback and changing requirements.

17.5. Core Concepts in Agile Project Management

Several key concepts underpin Agile methodologies:

a) Iterative Development: Projects are divided into small, manageable iterations (often called sprints), typically lasting 1-4 weeks.

b) Timeboxing: Each iteration and most Agile meetings are timeboxed, meaning they have a fixed duration.

c) Minimal Viable Product (MVP): The goal is to deliver a basic working version of the product as quickly as possible, then iteratively improve it.

d) User Stories: Requirements are captured as user stories, short descriptions of functionality from an end-user perspective.

e) Product Backlog: A prioritized list of all desired features and improvements for the product.

f) Continuous Integration and Delivery: Code changes are integrated frequently, and working software is delivered regularly.

g) Self-organizing Teams: Teams have the autonomy to determine how to best accomplish their work.

17.6. Benefits of Agile Project Management

Agile methodologies offer several advantages:

- Improved Product Quality: Regular testing and refinement lead to higher quality outcomes.

- Higher Customer Satisfaction: Continuous customer involvement ensures the product meets their needs.

- Increased Project Control: Frequent check-ins and adjustments keep the project on track.

- Reduced Risks: Early and regular delivery of working products reduces the risk of project failure.

- Faster Time to Market: The MVP approach allows for quicker product launches.

- Better Team Morale and Productivity: Self-organization and regular achievements boost team morale.

17.7. Challenges in Implementing Agile

Despite its benefits, Agile implementation can face several challenges:

- Organizational Resistance: Traditional organizations may struggle with the cultural shift required.

- Scaling Issues: Applying Agile principles to large projects or organizations can be complex.

- Documentation Concerns: The "just enough" documentation approach may not suffice for all industries.

- Regulatory Compliance: Some regulated industries may find it challenging to balance Agile with compliance requirements.

- Non-Software Contexts: While Agile originated in software development, adapting it to other fields can require creativity.

17.8. When to Use Agile (and When Not To)

Agile is particularly well-suited for projects where:
- Requirements are likely to change
- The end product is not clearly defined at the outset
- Regular customer feedback is crucial
- The project can be broken down into small, independent increments
However, traditional methods might be more appropriate when:
- Requirements are stable and well-understood from the beginning
- The project is simple and predictable

- Extensive documentation is required (e.g., in highly regulated industries)

- The customer prefers a fixed-price, fixed-scope contract

17.9. Summary

Agile project management represents a significant shift from traditional approaches, emphasizing flexibility, customer collaboration, and iterative development. Born out of the need for more adaptive methods in software development, Agile has since been adopted across various industries.

The Agile Manifesto and its twelve principles provide a foundation for Agile methodologies, promoting values such as individuals over processes, working products over documentation, collaboration over negotiation, and responsiveness to change.

While Agile offers numerous benefits, including improved product quality and customer satisfaction, it also presents challenges, particularly in traditional organizational structures. Understanding when to apply Agile methods – and when traditional approaches might be more suitable – is crucial for project success.

As we move forward, we'll explore specific Agile methodologies in more detail, providing you with a comprehensive toolkit for modern project management.

EIGHTEEN

SCRUM FRAMEWORK

18.1. Introduction to Scrum

Scrum is one of the most popular Agile frameworks, widely used in software development and increasingly adopted in other industries. Developed by Ken Schwaber and Jeff Sutherland in the early 1990s, Scrum provides a structured yet flexible approach to project management.

At its core, Scrum is built on empiricism, which asserts that knowledge comes from experience and making decisions based on what is observed. The three pillars of empiricism in Scrum are:

- Transparency: Significant aspects of the process must be visible to those responsible for the outcome.

- Inspection: Scrum users must frequently inspect Scrum artifacts and progress toward a goal to detect undesirable variances.

- Adaptation: If an inspector determines that one or more aspects of a process deviate outside acceptable limits, the process or the material being processed must be adjusted as quickly as possible.

18.2. Scrum Roles

Scrum defines three specific roles that form the Scrum Team:

a) Product Owner

- Responsible for maximizing the value of the product and the work of the Development Team.

- Manages the Product Backlog, including its content, availability, and ordering.

- Is the sole person responsible for managing the Product Backlog.

- Represents the stakeholders and is the voice of the customer.

Key responsibilities:

- Clearly expressing Product Backlog items

- Ordering the items in the Product Backlog to best achieve goals and missions

- Optimizing the value of the work the Development Team performs

- Ensuring that the Product Backlog is visible, transparent, and clear to all

b) Scrum Master

- Responsible for promoting and supporting Scrum as defined in the Scrum Guide.

- Helps everyone understand Scrum theory, practices, rules, and values.

Key responsibilities:

- Facilitating Scrum events as requested or needed

- Coaching the Development Team in self-organization and cross-functionality

- Helping the organization adopt Scrum

- Removing impediments to the Development Team's progress

- Ensuring that all Scrum events take place and are positive, productive, and kept within the timebox

c) Development Team

- Consists of professionals who do the work of delivering a potentially releasable Increment of "Done" product at the end of each Sprint.

- Self-organizing and cross-functional.

Key characteristics:

- Typically 3-9 members (excluding Scrum Master and Product Owner unless they are also executing the work of the sprint backlog)

- No titles for Development Team members, regardless of the work being performed by the person

- No sub-teams in the Development Team, regardless of domains that need to be addressed

- Individual Development Team members may have specialized skills and areas of focus, but accountability belongs to the Development Team as a whole

18.3. Scrum Artifacts

Scrum defines three primary artifacts:

a) Product Backlog

- An ordered list of everything that is known to be needed in the product.

- The single source of requirements for any changes to be made to the product.

- Constantly evolves as the product and environment in which it will be used changes.

Key aspects:

- Contains features, functions, requirements, enhancements, and fixes
- Items have attributes of a description, order, estimate, and value
- Often refined through the process of grooming or refinement

b) Sprint Backlog

- The set of Product Backlog items selected for the Sprint, plus a plan for delivering the product Increment and realizing the Sprint Goal.

- A forecast by the Development Team about what functionality will be in the next Increment and the work needed to deliver that functionality.

Key aspects:

- Makes visible all the work that the Development Team identifies as necessary to meet the Sprint Goal
- Includes at least one high priority process improvement identified in the previous Retrospective meeting
- Is a plan with enough detail that changes in progress can be understood in the Daily Scrum

c) Increment

- The sum of all the Product Backlog items completed during a Sprint and the value of the increments of all previous Sprints.

- Must be in useable condition regardless of whether the Product Owner decides to release it.

Key aspect:

- Definition of "Done": A shared understanding of what it means for work to be complete, ensuring transparency

18.4. Scrum Events

Scrum prescribes five events, all of which are timeboxed:

a) The Sprint

- A time-box of one month or less during which a "Done", useable, and potentially releasable product Increment is created.

- Has a consistent duration throughout a development effort.

- A new Sprint starts immediately after the conclusion of the previous Sprint.

Key aspects:

- Contains and consists of the Sprint Planning, Daily Scrums, the development work, the Sprint Review, and the Sprint Retrospective
- During the Sprint:

- No changes are made that would endanger the Sprint Goal
- Quality goals do not decrease
- Scope may be clarified and re-negotiated between the Product Owner and Development Team as more is learned

b) Sprint Planning
- Timeboxed to a maximum of eight hours for a one-month Sprint.
- Answers two questions:
- What can be delivered in the Increment resulting from the upcoming Sprint?
- How will the work needed to deliver the Increment be achieved?

Key outputs:
- Sprint Goal
- Sprint Backlog

c) Daily Scrum
- 15-minute time-boxed event for the Development Team to synchronize activities and create a plan for the next 24 hours.
- Held at the same time and place each day to reduce complexity.

Key aspects:
- Inspects progress toward the Sprint Goal
- Forecasts upcoming Sprint work
- Typically structured around three questions:
- What did I do yesterday that helped the Development Team meet the Sprint Goal?
- What will I do today to help the Development Team meet the Sprint Goal?
- Do I see any impediment that prevents me or the Development Team from meeting the Sprint Goal?

d) Sprint Review
- Held at the end of the Sprint to inspect the Increment and adapt the Product Backlog if needed.
- Timeboxed to a maximum of four hours for a one-month Sprint.

Key elements:
- The Scrum Team and stakeholders collaborate about what was done in the Sprint
- Presentation of the Increment to elicit feedback and foster collaboration
- Product Owner explains what Product Backlog items have been "Done" and what has not been "Done"

- Development Team discusses what went well during the Sprint, what problems it ran into, and how those problems were solved

- Review of the timeline, budget, potential capabilities, and marketplace for the next anticipated releases of functionality or capability of the product

e) Sprint Retrospective

- Opportunity for the Scrum Team to inspect itself and create a plan for improvements to be enacted during the next Sprint.

- Timeboxed to a maximum of three hours for a one-month Sprint.

Key purposes:

- Inspect how the last Sprint went with regards to people, relationships, process, and tools

- Identify and order the major items that went well and potential improvements

- Create a plan for implementing improvements to the way the Scrum Team does its work

18.5. Scrum in Practice

While the Scrum framework is straightforward, implementing it effectively requires practice and adaptation. Some key considerations for successful Scrum implementation include:

- Building a culture of trust and openness within the Scrum Team

- Ensuring all team members understand and embrace Agile and Scrum principles

- Properly empowering the Product Owner to make decisions about the product

- Supporting the Scrum Master in their role of servant-leadership

- Encouraging self-organization within the Development Team

- Maintaining a sustainable pace of work

- Continuously improving based on feedback and retrospectives

18.6. Scaling Scrum

As organizations grow and projects become more complex, scaling Scrum becomes necessary. Several frameworks exist for scaling Scrum, including:

- Scrum of Scrums: Multiple Scrum teams coordinate through representatives who attend a Scrum of Scrums meeting

- LeSS (Large-Scale Scrum): Maintains most of Scrum's practices while providing a framework for applying them at scale

- SAFe (Scaled Agile Framework): Provides a more prescriptive approach to scaling Agile practices across the enterprise

18.7. Common Challenges and Solutions

While Scrum can be highly effective, teams often face challenges in implementation:

- Challenge: Resistance to change

Solution: Gradual implementation, continuous education, and demonstrating early wins

- Challenge: Lack of stakeholder engagement

Solution: Regular demonstrations of progress, involving stakeholders in Sprint Reviews

- Challenge: Difficulty in estimating and planning

Solution: Use of relative estimation techniques like story points, and improving estimation through experience and retrospectives

- Challenge: Maintaining product quality

Solution: Incorporating quality practices into the Definition of Done, emphasis on technical excellence

- Challenge: Managing technical debt

Solution: Allocating time in Sprints for refactoring and improvements, making technical debt visible to stakeholders

18.8. Conclusion

Scrum provides a powerful framework for managing complex projects in an Agile manner. By embracing its roles, artifacts, and events, teams can deliver high-quality products that meet customer needs in a flexible and efficient way. However, it's important to remember that Scrum is a framework, not a prescriptive methodology. Each organization and team must adapt Scrum to their specific context while maintaining its core principles and values.

As we move forward, we'll explore other Agile methodologies that can complement or provide alternatives to Scrum, further expanding your Agile project management toolkit.

NINETEEN

OTHER AGILE METHODOLOGIES

19.1. Introduction

While Scrum is one of the most popular Agile methodologies, it's not the only one. This chapter explores other significant Agile methodologies that project managers should be familiar with. Each of these approaches offers unique perspectives and practices that can be valuable in different project contexts.

19.2. Kanban

Kanban, which means "visual sign" or "card" in Japanese, is a visual method for managing work as it moves through a process. Developed by Taiichi Ohno for Toyota manufacturing in the 1940s, it has since been adapted for knowledge work and software development.

Key Principles of Kanban:

a) Visualize the workflow

b) Limit Work in Progress (WIP)

c) Manage flow

d) Make process policies explicit

e) Implement feedback loops

f) Improve collaboratively, evolve experimentally

Kanban Board:

The central element of Kanban is the Kanban board, typically consisting of columns representing stages in a workflow (e.g., To Do, In Progress, Done). Work items, represented by cards, move across the board as they progress.

Benefits of Kanban:

- Flexibility: Can be applied to existing processes without significant changes
- Reduced waste: Limits WIP and identifies bottlenecks
- Continuous delivery: Focuses on flow of work rather than timeboxed iterations
- Visual management: Provides clear view of work status and progress

When to Use Kanban:
- For teams with a high volume of incoming requests
- In maintenance or support environments
- When priorities change frequently
- For teams transitioning from traditional to Agile methods

19.3. Extreme Programming (XP)

Extreme Programming, created by Kent Beck in the late 1990s, is an Agile methodology that emphasizes technical excellence and customer satisfaction.

Core Values of XP:
- Simplicity
- Communication
- Feedback
- Respect
- Courage

Key Practices of XP:

a) Pair Programming: Two programmers work together at one workstation

b) Test-Driven Development (TDD): Write tests before writing code

c) Continuous Integration: Integrate and test code changes frequently

d) Refactoring: Continuously improve code design without changing its behavior

e) Small Releases: Deliver working software frequently in short cycles

f) Collective Code Ownership: Anyone can change any part of the code

g) Coding Standards: Maintain consistent coding practices across the team

h) Sustainable Pace: Maintain a consistent, sustainable work rhythm

i) Whole Team: Include all contributors (developers, testers, business representatives) in the team

j) Planning Game: Combine business priorities and technical estimates to plan releases

Benefits of XP:

- High-quality code with fewer defects
- Increased productivity and faster delivery
- Improved team morale and collaboration
- Better alignment with customer needs

When to Use XP:
- For projects with changing requirements
- In environments that value technical excellence
- For teams with strong engineering practices
- When close customer collaboration is possible

19.4. Lean Software Development

Lean Software Development, adapted from Lean manufacturing principles by Mary and Tom Poppendieck, focuses on maximizing customer value while minimizing waste.

Seven Principles of Lean Software Development:

a) Eliminate Waste: Remove anything that doesn't add value

b) Build Quality In: Prevent defects rather than fixing them later

c) Create Knowledge: Continuously learn and improve

d) Defer Commitment: Make decisions at the last responsible moment

e) Deliver Fast: Provide value to customers quickly

f) Respect People: Empower and engage team members

g) Optimize the Whole: Focus on overall system performance, not local optimizations

Key Practices in Lean Software Development:
- Value Stream Mapping: Visualize and analyze the flow of value
- Kanban boards: Manage work in progress
- Continuous improvement (Kaizen): Regularly reflect and enhance processes
- Just-in-Time decisions: Make decisions when you have the most information
- Minimum Viable Product (MVP): Deliver the smallest product that provides value

Benefits of Lean:
- Reduced development time and costs
- Improved quality and customer satisfaction
- Enhanced team morale and productivity
- Better alignment with business goals

When to Use Lean:
- For organizations seeking to improve efficiency

- In projects where reducing waste is a priority
- When aiming to streamline decision-making processes
- For teams transitioning from traditional to Agile methods

19.5. Feature-Driven Development (FDD)

Feature-Driven Development, created by Jeff De Luca in 1997, is an iterative and incremental software development process that emphasizes delivering tangible, working software frequently.

Five Processes of FDD:

a) Develop an Overall Model

b) Build a Features List

c) Plan by Feature

d) Design by Feature

e) Build by Feature

Key Practices of FDD:

- Domain Object Modeling: Create an overall model of the system
- Development by Feature: Design and build by feature
- Individual Class (Code) Ownership: Assign clear ownership of code
- Feature Teams: Form small, dynamically created teams for each feature
- Inspections: Conduct design and code inspections
- Regular Build Schedule: Maintain a regular build and progress reporting rhythm

Benefits of FDD:

- Clear visibility of progress
- Early detection of errors
- Supports scalability for larger projects
- Emphasizes quality throughout the development process

When to Use FDD:

- For large-scale projects
- In organizations transitioning from traditional to Agile methods
- When clear documentation and reporting are required
- For teams with varying levels of experience

19.6. Dynamic Systems Development Method (DSDM)

DSDM is an Agile project delivery framework that focuses on delivering the right solution at the right time.

Eight Principles of DSDM:

a) Focus on the business need

b) Deliver on time

c) Collaborate

d) Never compromise quality

e) Build incrementally from firm foundations

f) Develop iteratively

g) Communicate continuously and clearly

h) Demonstrate control

Key Practices of DSDM:

- Timeboxing: Fixed time periods for delivery

- MoSCoW Prioritization: Must have, Should have, Could have, Won't have this time

- Iterative Development: Evolve the solution over time

- Facilitated Workshops: Collaborative sessions for rapid decision-making

Benefits of DSDM:

- Strong alignment with business objectives

- Emphasis on on-time delivery

- Clear prioritization of work

- Scalable for various project sizes

When to Use DSDM:

- For projects with fixed deadlines

- When strong business involvement is possible

- In organizations requiring a structured Agile approach

- For large-scale or complex projects

19.7. Crystal Methods

Crystal is a family of Agile methodologies developed by Alistair Cockburn. It emphasizes people over processes and is adaptable based on team size and project criticality.

Core Properties of Crystal:

- Frequent Delivery

- Reflective Improvement

- Close Communication

- Personal Safety

- Focus

- Easy Access to Expert Users

- Technical Environment with Automated Tests, Configuration Management, and Frequent Integration

Crystal variants (based on team size and project criticality):

- Clear: For teams of up to 8 people

- Yellow: For teams of 10-20 people

- Orange: For teams of 20-50 people
- Red: For teams of 50-100 people
Benefits of Crystal:
- Flexibility to adapt to different project types
- Focus on people and interactions
- Emphasis on continuous improvement
- Scalable for different team sizes
When to Use Crystal:
- For organizations wanting a people-centric approach
- When team dynamics and communication are priorities
- In environments where one-size-fits-all methodologies don't work
- For teams of varying sizes and project complexities

19.8. Conclusion

Each of these Agile methodologies offers unique strengths and is suited to different project contexts. While they share common Agile principles, they differ in their specific practices, terminology, and areas of emphasis.

The choice of methodology should be based on factors such as:
- Project characteristics and constraints
- Team size and composition
- Organizational culture and maturity
- Customer involvement and expectations
- Regulatory or compliance requirements

It's also worth noting that many organizations adopt hybrid approaches, combining elements from different methodologies to best suit their needs. The key is to understand the principles behind each approach and apply them thoughtfully to achieve the best outcomes for your projects and teams.

As you continue to explore and apply these methodologies, remember that Agile is not just about following practices, but about embracing a mindset of continuous improvement, collaboration, and delivery of value. The most successful Agile implementations are those that adapt these methodologies to their specific context while staying true to core Agile principles.

TWENTY
SCALING AGILE

20.1. Introduction to Scaling Agile

As organizations grow and projects become more complex, there's often a need to scale Agile practices beyond a single team. Scaling Agile involves applying Agile principles and practices across multiple teams, departments, or even the entire organization. This chapter explores the challenges of scaling Agile and introduces some of the most popular frameworks for addressing these challenges.

20.2. Challenges in Scaling Agile

Before diving into scaling frameworks, it's important to understand the common challenges organizations face when scaling Agile:

a) Coordination and dependencies: As the number of teams increases, managing dependencies and ensuring coordination becomes more complex.

b) Maintaining Agile culture: It can be difficult to maintain the Agile mindset and values across a larger organization.

c) Consistency vs. flexibility: Balancing the need for consistent practices with the flexibility to adapt to different team needs.

d) Governance and compliance: Ensuring proper governance and compliance without compromising Agility.

e) Tool integration: Integrating tools and processes across multiple teams and departments.

f) Organizational structure: Traditional hierarchical structures may not support Agile ways of working at scale.

g) Change management: Managing the organizational change required for large-scale Agile adoption.

20.3. Scaled Agile Framework (SAFe)

SAFe is one of the most popular frameworks for scaling Agile. Developed by Dean Leffingwell, it provides a structured approach for implementing Agile practices at enterprise scale.

Key components of SAFe:

a) Team Level: Incorporates Scrum, Kanban, and XP practices.

b) Program Level: Introduces the Agile Release Train (ART) concept, which aligns teams to a common mission.

c) Large Solution Level: Coordinates multiple ARTs working on a single solution.

d) Portfolio Level: Aligns execution to strategy and funds value streams.

Core values of SAFe:

- Alignment
- Built-in Quality
- Transparency
- Program Execution
- Leadership

Key practices:

- PI (Program Increment) Planning
- System Demo
- Inspect & Adapt
- DevOps and Continuous Delivery

When to use SAFe:

- For large enterprises with complex systems
- When a structured approach to scaling is needed
- In organizations with multiple interdependent teams

20.4. Large-Scale Scrum (LeSS)

LeSS, developed by Craig Larman and Bas Vodde, is a framework that extends Scrum to multiple teams working on a single product.

Two LeSS frameworks:

a) Basic LeSS: For 2-8 teams

b) LeSS Huge: For 8+ teams

Key principles of LeSS:

- Large-scale Scrum is Scrum
- Empirical process control
- Transparency
- More with less
- Whole-product focus
- Customer-centric

- Continuous improvement towards perfection

Key practices:

- Single Product Backlog
- Single Product Owner
- Sprint Planning with multiple teams
- Overall Retrospective

When to use LeSS:

- When scaling Scrum to multiple teams
- For organizations that want to maintain Scrum principles at scale
- When there's a single product with multiple teams

20.5. Disciplined Agile Delivery (DAD)

DAD, created by Scott Ambler and Mark Lines, is a hybrid approach that extends Scrum with strategies from other Agile methods.

Key components of DAD:

a) Foundation layer: Provides the philosophical and cultural base.

b) Disciplined DevOps layer: Focuses on the full delivery lifecycle.

c) Value Streams layer: Connects DAD to the rest of the organization.

d) Disciplined Agile Enterprise layer: Applies Agile and lean principles to all aspects of the enterprise.

Key principles:

- People-first
- Learning-oriented
- Full delivery lifecycle
- Goal-driven
- Enterprise awareness
- Choice is good

When to use DAD:

- For organizations wanting a flexible approach to scaling
- When a full-lifecycle approach is needed
- In complex environments with varying team needs

20.6. Spotify Model

While not a formal framework, the Spotify Model has gained popularity as an example of how to scale Agile in a flexible, culture-centric way.

Key components:

- Squads: Cross-functional, self-organizing teams (similar to Scrum teams)
- Tribes: Collections of squads working in related areas
- Chapters: Functional competency groups across squads

- Guilds: Communities of interest across the organization
Key principles:
- Autonomy
- Alignment
- Continuous improvement
- Cross-pollination of ideas
When to consider the Spotify Model:
- For organizations valuing flexibility and autonomy
- When a culture-first approach is preferred
- In creative or innovative environments

20.7. Scrum@Scale

Developed by Jeff Sutherland, co-creator of Scrum, Scrum@Scale is designed to scale Scrum across the entire organization.
Key components:
- Scrum of Scrums
- Executive Action Team
- Executive MetaScrum
Key principles:
- Scaled Daily Scrum
- Scaled Backlog Refinement
- Scaled Sprint Review
- Scaled Sprint Retrospective
When to use Scrum@Scale:
- For organizations already using Scrum
- When wanting to scale Scrum principles throughout the organization
- In environments needing a lightweight scaling approach

20.8. Nexus

Developed by Ken Schwaber, co-creator of Scrum, Nexus is a framework for scaling Scrum to multiple teams working on a single product.
Key components:
- Nexus Integration Team
- Nexus Sprint Planning
- Nexus Sprint Backlog
- Nexus Daily Scrum
- Nexus Sprint Review
- Nexus Sprint Retrospective
When to use Nexus:
- When scaling Scrum to 3-9 teams

- For organizations wanting a minimalistic approach to scaling
- When focusing on a single product with multiple teams

20.9. Choosing a Scaling Approach

Selecting the right scaling approach depends on various factors:

a) Organizational culture and readiness
b) Current Agile maturity
c) Size and complexity of projects/products
d) Industry and regulatory requirements
e) Desired level of prescriptiveness vs. flexibility

Steps for choosing and implementing a scaling approach:

1. Assess current state and needs
2. Educate leadership on scaling options
3. Start with a pilot or small-scale implementation
4. Gather feedback and adjust
5. Gradually expand adoption
6. Continuously improve and adapt the approach

20.10. Common Pitfalls in Scaling Agile

As organizations scale Agile, they often encounter several common pitfalls:

a) Focusing on practices over principles
b) Neglecting culture change
c) Insufficient leadership support
d) Inadequate training and coaching
e) Trying to scale too quickly
f) Ignoring team-level Agile fundamentals
g) Over-standardization across different contexts
h) Neglecting technical practices and architecture

20.11. Success Factors for Scaling Agile

To successfully scale Agile, organizations should focus on:

a) Strong leadership support and involvement
b) Investment in Agile training and coaching
c) Focus on cultural transformation
d) Emphasis on technical excellence and DevOps practices
e) Clear and frequent communication
f) Patience and persistence in the transformation process
g) Continuous improvement and adaptation of the scaling approach
h) Maintaining focus on customer value and outcomes

20.12. Conclusion

Scaling Agile is a complex undertaking that requires careful consideration of organizational context, culture, and goals. While frameworks provide valuable guidance, successful scaling often involves adapting and combining elements from different approaches to fit the specific needs of the organization.

Remember that scaling Agile is not just about processes and structures, but about extending Agile values and principles across the organization. It requires a commitment to continuous learning and improvement, and a willingness to challenge traditional ways of working.

As you embark on your Agile scaling journey, keep in mind that it's an iterative process. Start small, learn from your experiences, and gradually expand your Agile practices across the organization. With patience, persistence, and a focus on delivering value, you can successfully scale Agile to meet the needs of even the largest and most complex organizations.

TWENTY-ONE
HYBRID APPROACHES

21.1. Introduction to Hybrid Approaches

As organizations navigate the complexities of project management, many find that a single methodology doesn't always fit all scenarios. Hybrid approaches combine elements from different methodologies to create a tailored solution that addresses specific organizational needs. This chapter explores the concept of hybrid project management, focusing on combining traditional and Agile methods.

21.2. Understanding Hybrid Project Management

Hybrid project management is an approach that selectively combines elements of different project management methodologies. Most commonly, it involves blending traditional (often Waterfall) and Agile methods. The goal is to leverage the strengths of each approach while mitigating their respective weaknesses.

Key characteristics of hybrid approaches:
- Flexibility in methodology selection
- Customization to organizational needs
- Combination of predictive and adaptive elements
- Balance between structure and agility

21.3. Why Consider a Hybrid Approach?

Several factors may lead an organization to adopt a hybrid approach:

a) Complex projects with both predictable and unpredictable elements

b) Regulatory requirements that demand certain traditional practices

c) Organizational culture that's not ready for full Agile adoption

d) Projects with a mix of software and hardware components

e) Need to balance stakeholder expectations for both detailed planning and flexibility

f) Desire to gradually transition from traditional to Agile methods

21.4. Common Hybrid Models

While hybrid approaches can be highly customized, some common models have emerged:

a) Water-Scrum-Fall

- Initial planning and requirements gathering using Waterfall
- Development and testing using Scrum
- Final deployment and maintenance using Waterfall

b) Agile with a Waterfall Wrapper

- Overall project structure follows Waterfall phases
- Agile methods used within each phase for execution

c) Incremental Waterfall

- Project divided into increments, each following a Waterfall approach
- Allows for some flexibility and feedback between increments

d) Lean-Agile Hybrid

- Combines Lean principles with Agile practices
- Focuses on eliminating waste while maintaining agility

e) Scrumban

- Blends Scrum's structured sprints with Kanban's visual workflow management
- Useful for teams transitioning from Scrum to Kanban or vice versa

21.5. Designing a Hybrid Approach

Creating an effective hybrid approach involves several steps:

a) Assess project characteristics and organizational context

b) Identify which elements of different methodologies are most beneficial

c) Define how these elements will work together

d) Create a clear process flow and communication plan

e) Establish metrics for measuring success

f) Plan for regular review and adaptation of the approach

21.6. Key Components to Consider in a Hybrid Approach

When designing a hybrid approach, consider how to incorporate these key elements:

a) Project Initiation and Planning

- Level of upfront planning required
- Approach to requirements gathering and documentation

b) Team Structure and Roles

- Balance between specialized roles and cross-functional teams

- Adaptation of traditional and Agile roles (e.g., Project Manager vs. Scrum Master)

c) Work Breakdown and Estimation

- Use of Work Breakdown Structure (WBS) vs. Product Backlog
- Estimation techniques (e.g., function points vs. story points)

d) Scheduling and Timeboxing

- Balance between fixed schedules and iterative development
- Use of Gantt charts, sprints, or a combination

e) Progress Tracking and Reporting

- Metrics to track (e.g., earned value, velocity, burn-down charts)
- Frequency and format of status reports

f) Quality Management

- Integration of quality assurance throughout the process
- Balance between upfront planning and continuous testing

g) Change Management

- Process for handling change requests
- Balancing flexibility with scope control

h) Risk Management

- Proactive risk identification and mitigation strategies
- Continuous risk assessment and adaptation

21.7. Implementing a Hybrid Approach

Successfully implementing a hybrid approach requires careful planning and execution:

a) Educate stakeholders on the hybrid model

b) Provide training for team members on new processes and tools

c) Start with a pilot project to test and refine the approach

d) Establish clear communication channels and expectations

e) Regularly gather feedback and be prepared to adjust the approach

f) Ensure leadership support and commitment to the new model

21.8. Challenges in Hybrid Approaches

While hybrid approaches offer flexibility, they also come with challenges:

a) Complexity in process management

b) Potential confusion among team members about which practices to follow

c) Resistance from purists of either traditional or Agile methods

d) Difficulty in maintaining consistency across different projects

e) Risk of creating a "Frankenstein" process that inherits weaknesses from multiple methodologies

f) Challenges in tool selection and integration

21.9. Best Practices for Hybrid Project Management

To maximize the benefits of a hybrid approach:

a) Clearly define and communicate the hybrid process

b) Foster a culture of adaptability and continuous improvement

c) Prioritize effective communication and collaboration

d) Maintain focus on delivering value to stakeholders

e) Regularly review and refine the hybrid approach

f) Invest in proper training and change management

g) Ensure leadership support and alignment

h) Be prepared to adjust the balance between traditional and Agile elements as needed

21.10. Case Studies

To illustrate the application of hybrid approaches, consider including 2-3 detailed case studies. These should cover:

a) The organizational context and project characteristics

b) Why a hybrid approach was chosen

c) The specific hybrid model designed and implemented

d) Challenges faced and how they were overcome

e) Outcomes and lessons learned

21.11. Tools for Hybrid Project Management

Discuss tools that support hybrid approaches, such as:

a) Integrated project management platforms (e.g., Jira, Microsoft Project)

b) Visual management tools (e.g., Trello, Miro)

c) Collaboration and communication tools (e.g., Slack, Microsoft Teams)

d) Reporting and analytics tools for tracking diverse metrics

21.12. Future of Hybrid Approaches

Explore potential future trends in hybrid project management:

a) Increased customization and flexibility in methodologies

b) AI and machine learning in methodology selection and adaptation

c) Greater integration of DevOps practices in hybrid models

d) Evolution of project management tools to better support hybrid approaches

21.13. Conclusion

Hybrid project management approaches offer a flexible solution for organizations navigating the complex landscape of modern project delivery. By thoughtfully combining elements from different methodologies, organizations can create a tailored approach that leverages the strengths of both traditional and Agile methods.

The key to success with hybrid approaches lies in careful design, clear communication, and a willingness to adapt. As project environments continue to evolve, the ability to flexibly apply different methodological elements will become increasingly valuable.

Remember that there is no one-size-fits-all solution in project management. The most effective approach is one that is carefully tailored to your organization's specific needs, culture, and goals. By embracing a hybrid mindset, you can create a project management approach that is truly greater than the sum of its parts.

TWENTY-TWO
PROJECT MANAGEMENT TOOLS AND TECHNOLOGIES

22.1. Introduction to Project Management Tools

In today's digital age, project management tools and technologies play a crucial role in planning, executing, and monitoring projects. This chapter explores the landscape of project management software, collaboration tools, and emerging technologies that support both traditional and Agile methodologies.

22.2. Evolution of Project Management Tools

Brief history of project management tools:

- Early days: Manual tools like Gantt charts (1910s)

- 1950s-1970s: Emergence of PERT and CPM techniques

- 1980s: Introduction of personal computer-based project management software

- 1990s-2000s: Web-based tools and collaboration platforms

- 2010s onwards: Cloud-based solutions, mobile apps, and AI integration

22.3. Types of Project Management Tools

a) Scheduling and Planning Tools

- Features: Gantt charts, calendar views, resource allocation

- Examples: Microsoft Project, Oracle Primavera

b) Collaboration and Communication Tools

- Features: File sharing, messaging, video conferencing

- Examples: Slack, Microsoft Teams, Zoom

c) Task Management Tools
- Features: To-do lists, task assignments, progress tracking
- Examples: Asana, Trello, Todoist
d) Agile Project Management Tools
- Features: Backlog management, sprint planning, burndown charts
- Examples: Jira, VersionOne, Rally
e) All-in-One Project Management Platforms
- Features: Combination of scheduling, collaboration, and task management
- Examples: Monday.com, Basecamp, Wrike
f) Resource Management Tools
- Features: Capacity planning, resource allocation, workload management
- Examples: Float, Resource Guru
g) Risk Management Tools
- Features: Risk identification, assessment, and mitigation planning
- Examples: Active Risk Manager, Resolver
h) Time Tracking and Estimation Tools
- Features: Time logging, project time estimation, billing
- Examples: Toggl, Harvest

22.4. Key Features to Consider in Project Management Tools

When selecting a project management tool, consider the following features:
a) User Interface and Ease of Use
b) Customization Options
c) Reporting and Analytics
d) Integration Capabilities
e) Mobile Access
f) Collaboration Features
g) Security and Data Protection
h) Scalability
i) Cost and Licensing Model
j) Customer Support and Training Resources

22.5. Popular Project Management Software Solutions

Detailed overview of top project management tools, including:
a) Microsoft Project
- Strengths: Robust scheduling, resource management, integration with Office 365

- Weaknesses: Steep learning curve, can be complex for small projects

b) Jira

- Strengths: Excellent for Agile projects, customizable workflows, extensive integrations

- Weaknesses: Can be overwhelming for non-technical users

c) Trello

- Strengths: Intuitive Kanban-style interface, easy to use, good for small to medium projects

- Weaknesses: Limited features for complex project management

d) Asana

- Strengths: User-friendly, good for team collaboration, flexible project views

- Weaknesses: Can become cluttered with large projects, limited reporting

e) Monday.com

- Strengths: Visually appealing, highly customizable, good for various project types

- Weaknesses: Can be pricey for larger teams, learning curve for advanced features

f) Basecamp

- Strengths: Simple, all-in-one solution, good for client communication

- Weaknesses: Limited in advanced project management features

g) Wrike

- Strengths: Versatile, good for both Agile and traditional projects, strong reporting

- Weaknesses: Interface can be complex, higher price point

22.6. Collaboration and Communication Tools

Explore tools that support team collaboration and communication:

a) Slack

- Features: Channel-based messaging, file sharing, integrations

- Best for: Daily team communication, quick updates

b) Microsoft Teams

- Features: Chat, video calls, document collaboration, integration with Office 365

- Best for: Organizations heavily invested in Microsoft ecosystem

c) Zoom

- Features: Video conferencing, screen sharing, webinars

- Best for: Remote meetings, virtual events

d) Miro
- Features: Online whiteboard, brainstorming tools, templates
- Best for: Visual collaboration, design thinking sessions
e) Confluence
- Features: Knowledge base, team documentation, integration with Jira
- Best for: Creating and sharing team and project documentation

22.7. Agile-Specific Tools

Detailed look at tools designed specifically for Agile methodologies:
a) VersionOne
- Features: Portfolio management, release planning, sprint tracking
- Best for: Large-scale Agile implementations
b) Rally (now part of Broadcom)
- Features: Backlog management, iteration planning, SAFe support
- Best for: Enterprise-level Agile projects
c) Pivotal Tracker
- Features: Story management, velocity tracking, simple interface
- Best for: Small to medium-sized Agile teams
d) Taiga
- Features: Scrum and Kanban support, open-source
- Best for: Teams looking for a customizable, open-source solution

22.8. Emerging Technologies in Project Management

Explore how new technologies are shaping the future of project management:
a) Artificial Intelligence and Machine Learning
- Predictive analytics for project outcomes
- Automated scheduling and resource allocation
- Intelligent chatbots for project updates and queries
b) Virtual and Augmented Reality
- Virtual site visits and inspections
- Immersive project visualization
- Enhanced remote collaboration
c) Internet of Things (IoT)
- Real-time data collection from project sites
- Automated progress tracking
- Enhanced safety monitoring
d) Blockchain
- Secure contract management
- Transparent supply chain tracking

- Decentralized project governance

e) 5G Technology

- Enhanced real-time communication
- Improved remote work capabilities
- Support for IoT and AR/VR applications

22.9. Integrating Tools into Your Project Management Approach

Best practices for tool implementation:

a) Assess your organization's needs and project types

b) Involve key stakeholders in the selection process

c) Start with a pilot project or team

d) Provide adequate training and support

e) Regularly review and optimize tool usage

f) Be prepared to switch tools if needs change

22.10. Challenges in Adopting Project Management Tools

Common issues and how to address them:

a) Resistance to change

b) Integration with existing systems

c) Data migration from legacy tools

d) Ensuring data security and privacy

e) Balancing standardization with flexibility

f) Managing tool sprawl

22.11. Future Trends in Project Management Tools

Predictions for the evolution of project management technology:

a) Increased AI integration for decision support

b) Greater emphasis on remote collaboration features

c) More customizable and industry-specific solutions

d) Enhanced data analytics and visualization capabilities

e) Improved integration between different tools and platforms

22.12. Selecting the Right Tools for Your Organization

Framework for choosing appropriate project management tools:

a) Define your requirements and priorities

b) Evaluate multiple options against your criteria

c) Consider scalability and future needs

d) Assess total cost of ownership

e) Check for integration capabilities with existing systems

f) Trial tools before making a final decision

g) Plan for implementation and change management

22.13. Case Studies

Include 2-3 case studies of organizations successfully implementing project management tools, covering:

a) The organization's initial challenges

b) Tool selection process

c) Implementation strategy

d) Outcomes and benefits realized

e) Lessons learned

22.14. Conclusion

Project management tools and technologies are essential for modern project success. They enhance team collaboration, improve visibility into project progress, and enable more efficient resource management. However, it's crucial to remember that tools are enablers, not solutions in themselves. The key to successful project management still lies in sound methodologies, skilled team members, and effective leadership.

As technology continues to evolve, project managers must stay informed about new tools and trends. By thoughtfully selecting and implementing the right tools, organizations can significantly enhance their project management capabilities, leading to better outcomes and increased competitive advantage.

Remember, the best tool is one that fits your organization's specific needs, culture, and project types. Regular evaluation and willingness to adapt your toolset will ensure that your project management practices remain effective in an ever-changing business landscape.

TWENTY-THREE

THE FUTURE OF PROJECT MANAGEMENT

As we conclude our comprehensive exploration of project management basics and methodologies, it's crucial to reflect on the key learnings and look ahead to the future of this dynamic field.

23.1. **Recap of Key Concepts**

Throughout this book, we've covered a wide range of project management topics:

a) Traditional project management principles and methodologies

b) The Agile revolution and its various frameworks

c) Scaling Agile for larger organizations

d) Hybrid approaches that combine different methodologies

e) Tools and technologies supporting modern project management

These diverse approaches all aim to achieve the same fundamental goal: delivering successful projects that meet stakeholder needs efficiently and effectively.

23.2. **The Evolving Landscape of Project Management**

Project management is not a static field. It continues to evolve in response to:

a) Changing business environments

b) Technological advancements

c) Shifting workforce dynamics

d) Global economic trends

e) Emerging industries and sectors

As project managers, we must remain adaptable and open to new ideas and methodologies.

23.3. **Key Trends Shaping the Future of Project Management**

Several trends are likely to significantly impact project management in the coming years:

a) Increased Adoption of Agile and Hybrid Approaches

- Even traditionally plan-driven industries are incorporating Agile elements

- Hybrid approaches will become more sophisticated and tailored

b) Remote and Distributed Teams

- Global talent pools and changing work preferences are driving this trend

- Project management practices will need to adapt to virtual collaboration

c) Artificial Intelligence and Machine Learning

- AI will assist in decision-making, risk assessment, and resource allocation

- Predictive analytics will enhance project planning and execution

d) Emphasis on Soft Skills

- Technical skills remain important, but soft skills like leadership, communication, and emotional intelligence will be increasingly valued

e) Focus on Sustainability and Social Responsibility

- Projects will be evaluated not just on time, cost, and scope, but also on their environmental and social impact

f) Continuous Learning and Adaptation

- The rapid pace of change will require project managers to engage in lifelong learning

- Adaptability will be a key skill for future project managers

23.4. **Challenges and Opportunities**

As the field evolves, project managers will face both challenges and opportunities:

Challenges:

a) Keeping up with rapidly changing technologies

b) Managing increasingly complex and interdependent projects

c) Balancing competing methodologies and approaches

d) Ensuring data security in an increasingly digital environment

e) Navigating global and cultural complexities

Opportunities:

a) Leveraging new tools and technologies to enhance project outcomes

b) Developing innovative approaches to project management

c) Expanding the influence of project management across industries

d) Contributing to solving global challenges through effective project management

e) Shaping the future of work through project-based approaches

23.5. The Enduring Principles of Effective Project Management

Despite the changes and evolutions in the field, certain principles remain constant:

a) Clear Communication: The foundation of successful project management

b) Stakeholder Engagement: Understanding and meeting stakeholder needs

c) Risk Management: Proactively identifying and mitigating risks

d) Quality Focus: Ensuring project deliverables meet required standards

e) Continuous Improvement: Learning from each project to enhance future performance

f) Ethical Conduct: Maintaining integrity and professionalism in all aspects of project management

23.6. Advice for Aspiring and Practicing Project Managers

To thrive in this evolving field:

a) Embrace Lifelong Learning: Stay curious and open to new ideas and methodologies

b) Develop a Broad Skill Set: Combine technical, leadership, and domain-specific skills

c) Practice Adaptability: Be ready to adjust your approach based on project and organizational needs

d) Build Strong Networks: Connect with other professionals to share knowledge and experiences

e) Leverage Technology: Stay informed about and utilize appropriate tools and technologies

f) Maintain a Customer Focus: Always keep the end-user and project objectives in mind

g) Cultivate Emotional Intelligence: Develop your ability to understand and manage emotions in yourself and others

23.7. The Bigger Picture: Projects as Drivers of Change

As we conclude, it's important to recognize the broader impact of project management:

a) Economic Impact: Projects drive innovation, growth, and competitiveness across industries

b) Social Impact: Projects can address critical societal challenges and improve quality of life

c) Environmental Impact: Well-managed projects can contribute to sustainability efforts

d) Organizational Impact: Effective project management can transform organizational culture and capabilities

23.8. **Final Thoughts**

Project management is more than just a set of processes and tools – it's a discipline that drives progress and innovation across all sectors of society. As project managers, we have the opportunity and responsibility to lead positive change, deliver value, and shape the future.

The field of project management will continue to evolve, but its core purpose remains constant: to turn ideas into reality, to solve problems, and to create value. By mastering the fundamentals, staying adaptable, and embracing continuous learning, project managers can navigate the challenges and seize the opportunities that lie ahead.

As you move forward in your project management journey, remember that every project, regardless of its size or complexity, is an opportunity to make a difference. Approach each one with enthusiasm, integrity, and a commitment to excellence.

The future of project management is bright, filled with potential for innovation and positive impact. As project managers, we are at the forefront of this exciting future. Let's embrace it with confidence, creativity, and a steadfast commitment to delivering value through effective project management.

Thank you for embarking on this project management journey. We hope this book serves as a valuable resource as you navigate the exciting and rewarding world of project management. Best of luck in your future projects and career endeavours!

Glossary

A

Acceptance Criteria: Conditions that a project or product must satisfy to be accepted by a user, customer, or other stakeholder.

Agile: An iterative approach to software delivery that builds software incrementally from the start of the project, instead of trying to deliver it all at once near the end.

Agile Release Train (ART): A long-lived team of Agile teams, which, along with other stakeholders, incrementally develops, delivers, and where applicable operates, one or more solutions in a value stream.

Assumption: A factor in the planning process that is considered to be true, real, or certain without proof or demonstration.

B

Backlog: A prioritized list of features or tasks for a product or project.

Baseline: The approved time phased plan (for a project, a work package, or an activity), plus or minus approved project scope, cost, schedule and technical changes.

Bottom-up Estimating: A method of estimating project duration or cost by aggregating the estimates of lower-level components of the work breakdown structure.

Budget at Completion (BAC): The sum of all budgets established for the work to be performed on a project.

Burndown Chart: A graphical representation of work left to do versus time.

Business Case: A documented economic feasibility study used to establish validity of the benefits of a selected component lacking sufficient definition and that is used as a basis for the authorization of further project management activities.

C

Change Control: The process through which all requests to change the baseline scope of a project are captured, evaluated, and then approved, rejected, or deferred.

Constraint: A limiting factor that affects the execution of a project, program, portfolio, or process.

Critical Chain Method: A schedule network analysis technique that modifies the project schedule to account for limited resources.

Critical Path: The sequence of stages determining the minimum time needed for an operation, especially when analyzed on a computer for a large organization.

Critical Path Method (CPM): A technique used to predict project duration by analyzing which sequence of activities has the least amount of scheduling flexibility.

D

Daily Scrum: A 15-minute time-boxed event for the Development Team to synchronize activities and create a plan for the next 24 hours.

Deliverable: Any unique and verifiable product, result, or capability to perform a service that is required to be produced to complete a process, phase, or project.

Dependencies: The logical relationship between two or more activities in a project schedule.

DevOps: A set of practices that combines software development (Dev) and IT operations (Ops) aiming to shorten the systems development life cycle and provide continuous delivery with high software quality.

E

Earned Value (EV): The measure of work performed expressed in terms of the budget authorized for that work.

Earned Value Management (EVM): A project management technique for measuring project performance and progress in an objective manner.

Estimate: A quantitative assessment of the likely amount or outcome of a variable, such as project costs, resources, effort or durations.

Estimate at Completion (EAC): The expected total cost of completing all work expressed as the sum of the actual cost to date and the estimate to complete.

F

Fast Tracking: A schedule compression technique in which activities or phases normally done in sequence are performed in parallel for at least a portion of their duration.

Feasibility Study: An analysis of the viability of an idea through a logical and disciplined set of steps to assess an opportunity or problem, analyze alternatives, and recommend a solution.

Float (Slack): The amount of time that a task in a project network can be delayed without causing a delay to subsequent tasks or the project completion date.

G

Gantt Chart: A visual view of tasks scheduled over time.

Governance: The framework, functions, and processes that guide project management activities in order to create a unique product, service, or result to meet organizational strategic and operational goals.

I

Increment: In Scrum, a concrete stepping stone toward the Product Goal.

Issue: A point or matter in question or in dispute, or a point or matter that is not settled and is under discussion or over which there are opposing views or disagreements.

Iteration: A single development cycle, usually measured as one to four weeks in Agile methodologies.

K

Kanban: A visual system for managing work as it moves through a process.

Key Performance Indicator (KPI): A measurable value that demonstrates how effectively a company is achieving key business objectives.

Kickoff Meeting: A meeting held at the beginning of a project where the team and stakeholders meet to establish common understanding about the project.

L

Lean: A production practice that considers the expenditure of resources for any goal other than the creation of value for the end customer to be wasteful, and thus a target for elimination.

Lessons Learned: The learning gained from the process of performing the project.

M

Milestone: A significant point or event in a project.

Minimum Viable Product (MVP): A product with just enough features to satisfy early customers and provide feedback for future product development.

Mitigation: A risk response strategy whereby the project team acts to decrease the probability of occurrence or impact of a risk.

Monte Carlo Analysis: A technique that computes or iterates the project cost or schedule many times using input values selected at random from probability distributions of possible costs or durations, to calculate a distribution of possible outcomes.

N

Network Diagram: A schematic display of the logical relationships among project activities.

O

Opportunity: A risk that would have a positive effect on one or more project objectives.

P

PERT (Program Evaluation and Review Technique): A method of analyzing the tasks involved in completing a project, especially the time needed to complete each task, and identifying the minimum time needed to complete the total project.

PMBOK (Project Management Body of Knowledge): A set of standard terminology and guidelines for project management.

Portfolio: Projects, programs, sub-portfolios, and operations managed as a group to achieve strategic objectives.

Product Backlog: An ordered list of everything that is known to be needed in the product.

Product Owner: The person responsible for maximizing the value of the product resulting from work of the Development Team.

Program: A group of related projects managed in a coordinated way to obtain benefits and control not available from managing them individually.

Project Charter: A document that formally authorizes the existence of a project and provides the project manager with the authority to apply organizational resources to project activities.

Project Life Cycle: The series of phases that a project passes through from its initiation to its closure.

Project Management Office (PMO): A management structure that standardizes the project-related governance processes and facilitates the sharing of resources, methodologies, tools, and techniques.

Q

Quality Assurance (QA): The process of evaluating overall project performance on a regular basis to provide confidence that the project will satisfy the relevant quality standards.

R

RACI Chart: A matrix of all the activities or decision-making authorities undertaken in an organization set against all the people or roles.

Risk: An uncertain event or condition that, if it occurs, has a positive or negative effect on one or more project objectives.

Risk Management: The process of identifying, analyzing and responding to risk factors throughout the life of a project.

S

Scaled Agile Framework (SAFe): A set of organization and workflow patterns intended to guide enterprises in scaling lean and agile practices.

Scope: The sum of the products, services, and results to be provided as a project.

Scrum: An Agile framework for completing complex projects.

Scrum Master: The person responsible for ensuring Scrum is understood and enacted.

Sprint: A set period of time during which specific work has to be completed and made ready for review in Scrum methodology.

Stakeholder: An individual, group, or organization who may affect, be affected by, or perceive itself to be affected by a decision, activity, or outcome of a project.

T

Task: An activity that needs to be accomplished within a defined period of time or by a deadline.

Triple Constraint: The combination of the three most significant restrictions on any project: scope, schedule and cost.

U

User Story: A very high-level definition of a requirement, containing just enough information so that the developers can produce a reasonable estimate of the effort to implement it.

V

Velocity: A measure of the amount of work a Team can tackle during a single Sprint.

W

Waterfall Model: A linear sequential approach to software development that follows a specific flow.

Work Breakdown Structure (WBS): A deliverable-oriented hierarchical decomposition of the work to be executed by the project team.

This glossary covers a wide range of project management terms, from traditional to Agile methodologies, and includes some more advanced concepts.

Refrences

Agile Alliance. (2021). Agile Manifesto. https://www.agilealliance.org/agile101/the-agile-manifesto/

Beck, K., et al. (2001). Manifesto for Agile Software Development. https://agilemanifesto.org/

Cohn, M. (2004). User Stories Applied: For Agile Software Development. Addison-Wesley Professional.

Project Management Institute. (2021). A Guide to the Project Management Body of Knowledge (PMBOK® Guide) – Seventh Edition. Project Management Institute, Inc.

Schwaber, K., & Sutherland, J. (2020). The Scrum Guide. https://scrumguides.org/scrum-guide.html

Stellman, A., & Greene, J. (2014). Learning Agile: Understanding Scrum, XP, Lean, and Kanban. O'Reilly Media.

Kerzner, H. (2017). Project Management: A Systems Approach to Planning, Scheduling, and Controlling. John Wiley & Sons.

Leffingwell, D. (2018). SAFe 4.5 Reference Guide: Scaled Agile Framework for Lean Enterprises. Addison-Wesley Professional.

Larman, C., & Vodde, B. (2016). Large-Scale Scrum: More with LeSS. Addison-Wesley Professional.

Anderson, D. J., & Carmichael, A. (2016). Essential Kanban Condensed. Blue Hole Press.

Ries, E. (2011). The Lean Startup: How Today's Entrepreneurs Use Continuous Innovation to Create Radically Successful Businesses. Crown Business.

Womack, J. P., & Jones, D. T. (2003). Lean Thinking: Banish Waste and Create Wealth in Your Corporation. Free Press.

Goldratt, E. M., & Cox, J. (2004). The Goal: A Process of Ongoing Improvement. North River Press.

Brooks, F. P. (1995). The Mythical Man-Month: Essays on Software Engineering. Addison-Wesley Professional.

DeMarco, T., & Lister, T. (2013). Peopleware: Productive Projects and Teams. Addison-Wesley Professional.

Highsmith, J. (2009). Agile Project Management: Creating Innovative Products. Addison-Wesley Professional.

Sutherland, J. (2014). Scrum: The Art of Doing Twice the Work in Half the Time. Crown Business.

Kim, G., Debois, P., Willis, J., & Humble, J. (2016). The DevOps Handbook: How to Create World-Class Agility, Reliability, and Security in Technology Organizations. IT Revolution Press.

Rubin, K. S. (2012). Essential Scrum: A Practical Guide to the Most Popular Agile Process. Addison-Wesley Professional.

Cockburn, A. (2006). Agile Software Development: The Cooperative Game. Addison-Wesley Professional.

Online Resources:

Agile Alliance: https://www.agilealliance.org/

Scrum.org: https://www.scrum.org/

Scaled Agile Framework (SAFe): https://www.scaledagileframework.com/

Project Management Institute: https://www.pmi.org/

International Project Management Association: https://www.ipma.world/

Kanban University: https://kanban.university/

Lean Enterprise Institute: https://www.lean.org/

DevOps Institute: https://devopsinstitute.com/

Agile Manifesto: https://agilemanifesto.org/

Scrum Alliance: https://www.scrumalliance.org/